San Antonio's
PASSPORT TO FUN

Denise Barkis Richter, Ph.D.

Library of Congress Control Number: 2023915801

ISBN: 979-8-9888787-1-1

Text and photos by Denise Barkis Richter, Ph.D.

Cover design and illustration by Aedan Richter

Image on page iii by Aedan Richter

Back cover image by Pableaux Johnson

Printed in the United States of America

Please note that websites, phone numbers, addresses, and companies are subject to change, cancellation, or closure. I did my best to relay the most accurate information available, so please do not hold me liable for incorrect information.

DEDICATION

To my fellow San Antonio, Texas, bloggers; my fellow guides in the Professional Tour Guide Association of San Antonio; my teachers; my former students and colleagues; my friends; my mother and father; my siblings; my BFF Amy; and especially my husband and daughter, who let me photograph their food before they dig in.

TABLE OF CONTENTS

PREFACE

I love to travel, and I love to write about traveling. Because my gallivanting budget is limited, I decided to become a tourist in my own town, San Antonio, Texas, which happens to be one of the most beautiful, historic, and romantic cities on the planet.

I've been writing about fun things to do and see in the Alamo City on my blog, sanantoniotourist.net, since 2010. (Please follow me on Facebook at facebook.com/SanAntonioTourist for the latest!) It makes me happy to receive comments from San Antonio natives who discovered something new through my blog or from visitors who thank me for helping them plan a memorable visit.

I moved to San Antonio in 1979 as an 18-year-old freshman in college, and I have grown to love my adopted city. I hope that some of my *amor* for the Alamo City rubs off on you.

It is my sincerest wish that both visitors and natives will use this book as your passport to fun! Each time you experience one of the 101 things, write the day you did it in the margin along with who accompanied you, and a favorite memory. This "passport" will become a treasured keepsake.

¡Disfrute! (Enjoy!) ¡Viva San Antonio!

1

REMEMBER THE ALAMO

Once while I was traveling through Ireland, my bus driver confessed that he played hooky every time John Wayne's 1960 movie "The Alamo" came on TV. Though the historic mission is tiny in person, its reputation is grand throughout the world. It's the number one travel destination in Texas, and it and San Antonio's four other eighteenth-century Spanish colonial missions are a UNESCO World Heritage Site, the only one in Texas and one of only twenty-four in the U.S. On the Ireland trip, I happened to have a faux coonskin cap with me, and I gave it to the teary-eyed driver. Yes, the Alamo delivers that kind of emotional impact. Don't miss it. Entry now requires a free, timed ticket. Reserve yours online.

300 Alamo Plaza
(210) 225-1391
thealamo.org

2
MEANDER ALONG THE RIVER WALK

San Antonio's River Walk, also known as the Paseo del Rio, on the San Antonio River is one of the most beautiful spots in the United States. No brag, just fact. Ask anyone who's been. The day after Thanksgiving through the Feast of the Epiphany in early January has always been my favorite time of year in downtown San Antonio. Twinkle lights in the trees along the River Walk create a magical space that transports you into a different realm. Strolling along the Paseo del Rio in a sea of lights will put even the grinchiest of grinches in a good mood. Throughout the year, you will also enjoy experiencing the river being dyed green for St. Patrick's Day, the Fiesta River Parade, Spurs championship parades, arts & crafts fairs, restaurants, bars, clubs, and shopping, all thanks to the feisty women of the San Antonio Conservation Society and Architect Robert H.H. Hugman, whose 1929 proposal saved the river from being paved over and used as a storm sewer. Works Progress Administration funds post-Depression sealed the deal. Thank you, FDR.

(210) 244-2051
thesanantonioriverwalk.com

3

SIT FOR A SPELL IN
SAN FERNANDO CATHEDRAL

Many believe that the Alamo is the heart of San Antonio, but in reality San Fernando Cathedral wears that crown. Built by the Canary Islands settlers in 1738, a 1828 fire destroyed the church. In 1872, its dome fell in, and in 1921, floodwaters reached as high as the Stations of the Cross. Despite all of these setbacks, the cathedral, which underwent a major restoration in 2003, remained strong. Jim Bowie was married in San Fernando, and his remains are entombed there along with those of Davy Crockett and William B. Travis. Thanks to the leadership of Phil Hardberger, a former San Antonio mayor, the area in front of San Fernando Cathedral is now a pedestrian-only plaza that leads down to the River Walk. The cathedral and its surrounding area are definitely on my Top Ten San Antonio must-see destinations. When Pope John Paul II was in San Antonio in 1987 and celebrated Mass at San Fernando, he said that he knew he was in the U.S., but he felt that he was in Mexico. He was. The Mexican and Spanish roots of San Antonio are deepest at San Fernando. Don't miss San Antonio | The Saga, a glorious 24-minute, 7,000-square foot multimedia art exhibit of San Antonio's history that is projected onto the cathedral on Tuesdays through Sundays at 9 p.m. and at 9:30 p.m.

115 Main Plaza
archsa.org/parishes/san-fernando-cathedral

4
TAKE IN SAN ANTONIO'S ART
MUSEUMS AND GALLERIES

The Alamo City is blessed with an abundance of art museums and galleries. ARTE ES VIDA (ART IS LIFE) is a bumper sticker you'll see around town. No need to travel to Los Angeles, New York City, London, Paris or Rome. Chances are we have something by your favorite artist or from your favorite time period right here!

- Artpace Contemporary Art Gallery
445 N. Main Ave.
(210) 212-4900
artpace.org
- Blue Star Contemporary Art Museum
116 Blue Star
(210) 227-6960
bluestarart.org
- Briscoe Western Art Museum
210 W. Market Street
(210) 299-4499
briscoemuseum.org
- Centro de Artes
101 S. Santa Rosa Ave. in Historic Market Square
(210) 207-1436
getcreativesanantonio.com/Galleries/Centro-de-Artes

- Culture Commons Gallery
115 Plaza de Armas
(210) 206-2787
getcreativesanantonio.com/Galleries/Culture-Commons
- McNay Art Museum
6000 N. New Braunfels Ave.
(210) 824-5368
mcnayart.org
- Ruby City
150 Camp St.
(210) 227-8400
rubycity.org
- San Antonio Museum of Art
200 W. Jones Ave.
(210) 978-8100
samuseum.org

5
BECOME A BREAKFAST TACO BELIEVER

Whenever I travel outside of San Antonio, I most enjoy returning home to breakfast tacos. Those who live here get it. Those who don't live here don't know what they're missing. San Antonio, Texas, is not only the capital of Tex-Mex cuisine, but it is the undisputed capital of breakfast tacos. It's no surprise that Victor Wembanyama, the Spurs' 2023 first-choice draft pick, announced that he was excited about moving to San Antonio for its breakfast tacos. We have an embarrassment of riches. Corn or flour tortillas? Eggs or not? Potatoes? Bacon, ham or sausage? With or without cheese? Barbacoa? Chorizo? Guacamole? So many options. Personally, I find a chilaquiles taco with grated cheese on a corn tortilla and the perfect amount of salsa quemada to be a life-affirming experience.

A Baker's Dozen of Breakfast Taco Picks

- Blue Moon Cafe
  facebook.com/BlueMoonMexRestaurant
- Chela's
  facebook.com/chelastacosalamoheights
- Maria's Café
  facebook.com/mariascafe.ann
- El Milagrito Cafe
  elmilagritocafe.com
- Mendez Café
  facebook.com/pages/Mendez-Cafe/
  1401964606743670
- Panchito's Mexican Restaurant
  panchitos.net
- Pete's Tako House
  petestakohouse.com
- Sabor de Mexico
  facebook.com/pages/Sabor-De-Mexico/
  114055505293224
- Taco Cabana
  tacocabana.com
- Taco House
  facebook.com/tacohousesa
- Taco Taco Café
  tacotacosa.com
- Teka Molino
  tekamolino.com
- Tia's Taco Hut
  tiastacohuttx.com

6

VISIT TEXAS' ONLY UNESCO WORLD HERITAGE SITE

San Antonio, first called Yanaguana by the Payayan Indians thousands of years ago, was renamed San Antonio in 1691 when Spanish explorers came upon the river on the saint's feast day, June 13. The eighteenth-century Spanish Colonial Missions —Concepción, San José, San Juan Capistrano, Espada, and San Antonio de Valero, the Alamo—are one of only twenty-four World Heritage Sites in the United States. They share the list with the Grand Canyon, Yellowstone, the Statue of Liberty and Monticello. In other words, they are a MUST DO thing in San Antonio. Though similar, each mission has its own distinct flavor. Noteworthy items include the Rose Window and grist mill at San José, the arched doorway and aqueduct at Espada, the cloister at Concepción, the demonstration garden at San Juan, and the shrine and Long Barrack at the Alamo. The national park's Visitor Center is located at San José, where the 20-minute film "Gente de Razon" explains life in the 1700s. The Mission Reach, an 8-mile stretch of the River Walk, makes traveling from mission to mission a breeze. The Archdiocese of San Antonio now offers El Camino de San Antonio Missions, a partnership with Spain's Camino de Santiago de Compostela, for pilgrims of all faiths (or no faith) who would like to renew their spirit while journeying from mission to mission.

nps.gov/saan/index and thealamo.org
archsa.org/caminosanantonio

7
ATTEND ONE OF SAN ANTONIO'S LIFE-AFFIRMING FESTIVALS

Music. Food. Dancing. Fun! We're San Antonio, and you're invited to celebrate the fabulousness that is the Alamo City all year round.

Asian Festival: asianfestivalsa.org

Balcones Heights Jazz Festival: facebook.com/BalconesHeightsJazzFestival

Barbacoa & Big Red Festival: facebook.com/BarbacoaBigRedFestival

Black History Film Series: sacaam.org

Cactus Pear Music Festival: cpmf.us

CarFestSA: carfestsa.org

CelebrateSA: saparks.org/event/celebrate-sa

Chalk It Up: artpace.org/chalk-it-up

Cinco de Mayo: facebook.com/marketsquaresa

CineFestival: guadalupeculturalarts.org/cine-festival

Día de los Muertos: facebook.com/marketsquaresa

Diez y Seis: facebook.com/marketsquaresa

Diwali Festival of Lights: diwalisa.com

Fiesta: fiestasanantonio.org

Fotoseptiembre: fotoseptiembreusa.com

Fourth of July Celebration: saparks.org/event/fourth-of-july-celebration

Irish Festival: harpandshamrock.org

Jazz'SAlive: saparksfoundation.org/events/jazzsalive

Jewish Film Festival: jccsanantonio.org/filmfestival

Lebanese Food Festival: stgeorgesa.org/post/15-annual-lebanese-food-festival

Luminaria: luminariasa.org

Mariachi Extravaganza: mariachimusic.com

Oktoberfest: facebook.com/the.Beethoven

Pride Festival: pridesanantonio.org/pride-festival

Puerto Rican Festival: coquisa.org

San Antonio Beer Festival: sanantoniobeerfestival.com

San Antonio Book Festival: sabookfestival.org

San Antonio Coffee Festival: sacoffeefest.com

San Antonio Film Festival: safilm.com

San Antonio Folklife and Dance Festival: safdf.org

San Antonio Tango Festival: sanantoniotangofestival.com

Tasting Texas Wine + Food Festival: culinariasa.org/tastingtexas

Tejano Conjunto Festival: guadalupeculturalarts.org/tejano-conjunto-festival

Third Coast Rhythm Project Annual Tap Festival: thirdcoastrhythm.com/about-the-festival

World Heritage Festival: worldheritagefestival.org

8

TRANSPORT YOURSELF INTO ANOTHER WORLD AT THE MAJESTIC THEATRE

Some of the best concerts I've ever attended were in the Majestic Theater: Stevie Ray Vaughan, James Taylor, Sade, Kenny Loggins, Basia, Little Feat, ZZ Top, and Tony Bennett, to name just a few. In addition, I've thrilled to the traveling Broadway shows of *The Lion King, Cats, Wicked, Annie, 12 Angry Men, Beauty and the Beast, On Your Feet!,* and *Beautiful* at the Majestic. Some of the movie *Selena* with Jennifer Lopez was filmed here. Yes, performing artists draw patrons into this 2,300-seat theatre, but the venue itself is another draw. The 1929 Mediterranean-style theatre designed by John Eberson is an over-the-top Baroque fantasy that's listed on the National Register of Historic Places and is a National Historic Landmark. I get a charge every time I walk through the Majestic's doors. I never tire of checking out the fish in the aquarium, people-watching in the multi-level atrium, and gazing up at the ceiling's twinkling stars. If you haven't been to the Majestic or haven't been in awhile, what are you waiting on?

224 East Houston Street
(210) 226-5700
majesticempire.com

9

TAKE IN A SPURS GAME AT THE FROST BANK CENTER

When a friend of mine was in Madrid, Spain, he and his family wandered into a prohibited military area in the center of the city. Before they realized their mistake, the Guardia Civil, the city's police force, surrounded them. My friend, a former Marine who speaks Spanish, raised his hands over his head and said, "Lo siento. No somos de aqui. Somos de San Antonio, Texas." (We're sorry. We're not from here. We're from San Antonio, Texas.) One of the guards smiled and replied, "Los Spurs!" Yes, the San Antonio Spurs have put the Alamo City on the world's map. With an international set of players along with those from the U.S., the National Basketball Association champions make San Antonio proud. Coach Gregg "Pop" Popovich, has brought out the best in the team since 1996, winning five NBA championships. Pop was recognized as the NBA's coach with the most wins in 2019. From the end of October through April, don't miss your opportunity to witness the Spurs in action.

(210) 444-5000
nba.com/spurs/tickets

10
ESCAPE INTO NATURE AT
BRACKENRIDGE PARK

Brackenridge Park is one of San Antonio's rejuvenating urban oases. Minutes from the center of downtown, you will find yourself surrounded by tall trees and a less-traveled stretch of the San Antonio River. Founded in 1899, the 344-acre park underwent a major renovation in 2004, thanks to the Junior League of San Antonio, and three walking trails opened to the public: Waterworks (1.5 miles), Wildlife (1 mile), and Wilderness (.75 miles). Public art is located along each trail, and inviting picnic tables dot the landscape. While there, don't miss Dionicio Rodriguez's 1926 faux bois ("false wood") footbridge. When you need a place to clear your head and commune with some koi, head to the park's sunken gardens, officially named the San Antonio Japanese Tea Garden. The San Antonio Zoo and its miniature trains are also located in the park. You can make your visit a two-for one (gardens/park), three-for-one (gardens/park/zoo), or four-for-one (gardens/park/zoo/ miniature train) adventure. Notice, however, the gardens are a given. Do not miss them! Plus, you won't have to shell out any dinero. Admission to the gardens is free.

3700 N. St. Mary's
(210) 207-8480
sanantonio.gov/parksandrec

11
BROWSE THE ALAMO CITY'S
PUBLIC LIBRARIES

For those of us with children who've watched the "Spy Kids" movies written and directed by San Antonio native Robert Rodriguez, you'll recognize San Antonio's Central Library in downtown San Antonio as the OSS headquarters in SK2. Designed by Mexican architect Ricardo Legoretta, the edifice is known for its enchilada red exterior. Inside you'll find computers with free Internet connectivity; a comfortable place to cool off while you peruse magazines and books; an art gallery; a Dale Chihuly glass sculpture titled Fiesta Tower; a Fernando Botero horse sculpture; and a mural by esteemed San Antonio artist Jesse Treviño. San Antonio boasts 29 branch libraries scattered throughout the city in addition to the Central Library. Landa Branch Library, housed in a 1920s Mediterranean-styled mansion at 233 Bushnell, is my favorite. Be sure to enjoy the Carlos Cortés-designed *faux bois* pavilion in the garden while you're there.

600 Soledad
(210) 207-2500
mysapl.org

12
GET YOUR SCARE ON IN
DOWNTOWN SAN ANTONIO

Spirits of those who died during the Battle of the Alamo, hotel housekeepers who met an untimely end but are still driven to tidy up, and Captain Richard King, founder of the King Ranch, are all apparitions that you might encounter while on a ghost tour of downtown San Antonio. For those of us who've lived here for awhile, tales of La Llorona, the Donkey Lady, and the haunted railroad tracks on the South Side abound, so sign up for a Candlelight Ghost Tour by the Sisters Grimm while you're in town to see if you might stumble upon the supernatural. The sisters, descendants of San Antonio's Canary Islands founders, weave tales of the city's history throughout the nightly hour and a half walking tour that covers the Alamo, the Menger Hotel, the Emily Morgan Hotel, San Fernando Cathedral, the Bexar County Courthouse, the Spanish Governor's Palace, the O. Henry House, and Casa Navarro over approximately 2.5 miles.

300 Alamo Plaza
(210) 638-1338
sistersgrimmghosttour.com

13
WITNESS THE PASSION OF THE CHRIST

For more than 30 years, the streets of downtown San Antonio have become a living reminder of Jesus' painful final hours before his death on the cross. Every Good Friday—the Friday before Easter Sunday—actors playing Jesus, Mary, Mary Magdalene, Simon, Veronica, Pilate, Roman soldiers, and more walk from Milam Park to Main Plaza, reenacting the trial, crowning with thorns, and crucifixion of Jesus. Parishioners of San Fernando Cathedral stage this annual event, giving those along the Via Crucis—the Way of Sorrows—a palpable sense of Christ's suffering. The volunteers' hope is to inspire those who attend and those who act out the roles to deepen their faith in God.

sfcathedral.org/via-crucis

14
STROLL THROUGH HISTORIC LA VILLITA

San Antonio's La Villita (little village) is the city's original melting pot. Native Americans, Mexicans, Spaniards, East Texans, Texas Rangers, Germans, Swiss, French and Anglos all called this little piece of land home. Located in the shadow of the Hilton Palacio del Rio along the banks of the San Antonio River on South Alamo at Nueva Streets, La Villita's melting pot heritage lives on today through the countless festivals that are held here each year: Night in Old San Antonio, Diwali: Festival of Light, St. Patrick's Day Festival, Fiesta Noche del Rio, and Día de Los Muertos, to name a few. If you aren't in town for one of these festivals, don't worry. The artisan shops, galleries, restaurants, and Little Church of La Villita offer plenty to do and see.

418 Villita Street
(210) 207-8614
lavillitasanantonio.com

15

IMAGINE LATE 19TH CENTURY LIFE IN KING WILLIAM

Surely the spirit of Walter Nold Mathis still roams the dazzling rooms and lovely grounds of his beloved Villa Finale, a grand 1876-Italianate home in San Antonio's King William neighborhood, the first historic neighborhood in Texas. Even if Mathis' spirit doesn't ramble around, his essence definitely lingers on through his immense collection of fine and decorative arts. The Villa Finale is the first National Trust Historic Site in the State of Texas, and Mathis left plenty behind for visitors to peruse: Napoleonic memorabilia, including a death mask of the French emperor; snuff and match boxes; letter openers; Greek and Russian religious items; sterling silver coffee and tea sets; pewter plates, mugs and serving pieces; prints by the artist Mary Bonner; bronze statues; Italian paintings; more than 2,000 books; English Wedgwood; and on and on. Villa Finale is a wonderful example of the magnificent homes in this historic neighborhood built by German immigrants.

ourkwa.org/places
villafinale.org

16
LEAVE YOUR WORRIES BEHIND AT OUR LADY OF LOURDES GROTTO

San Antonio's Our Lady of Lourdes Grotto is the perfect space to take a deep breath away from life's hustle and bustle. Plus, it's a two-for-one grotto. Besides the Lourdes grotto, an exact replica of the shrine in France, you may also visit the Our Lady of Guadalupe Tepeyac de San Antonio place of prayer and devotion located on top of the Lourdes grotto. Masses at the grotto are Saturdays at 6 p.m. in Spanish; Sundays at 9 a.m. in English and 11:30 a.m. in Spanish; Mondays through Saturdays at 7 a.m. in English; and Mondays through Fridays at noon in Spanish. The rosary is said at 7:30 p.m. on Mondays and Wednesdays. The Oblate School of Theology's five acres of grounds are filled with walking paths, shade trees, outdoor Stations of the Cross and benches. A large gift shop, filled with reasonably priced books, holy medals, holy cards and rosaries, is located near the grotto and is open seven days a week.

5712 Blanco Road, between Oblate and Parade
(210) 342-9864
ost.edu/lourdes-grotto-guadalupe-tepeyac

17

SAUNTER ALONG SAN PEDRO CREEK CULTURE PARK

San Antonio's 2018 Tricentennial Celebration was not just a giant three-hundredth birthday party. It was also an opportunity for current citizens to leave behind something significant—a legacy—for future generations to enjoy. Thanks to the vision and planning of Bexar County's leaders, the City of San Antonio, and the San Antonio River Authority, the San Pedro Creek Culture Park opened near Columbus Park on the western edge of downtown, transforming an ugly drainage ditch into a restored ecosystem that celebrates San Antonio's vibrant history. ADA-accessible walkways allow visitors to stroll past site-specific artwork created by local artists and writers that reveals San Pedro Creek's long history. When complete, the linear park will have added four miles of walking trails and 11 acres of landscaping to the heart of downtown.

715 Camaron Street
spcculturepark.com

18
PAY YOUR RESPECTS AT SAN ANTONIO'S HISTORIC CEMETERIES

In 1853, the City of San Antonio purchased twenty acres east of downtown to house the final remains of San Antonio's citizens. By 1904, thirty-one public, private, religious, fraternal, and military cemeteries covered more than 103 acres. Many of San Antonio's "Who's Who" are buried here: Clara Driscoll and Adina De Zavala, saviors of the Alamo; John Lang Sinclair, songwriter of "The Eyes of Texas;" Julian Onderdonk, Texas landscape artist; Samuel Augustus Maverick, a lawyer, politician and signer of the Texas Declaration of Independence; Alfred Giles, architect; Thomas Claiborne Frost, founder of Frost Bank; Harry M. Wurzbach, Congressman; and Robert H.H. Hugman, concept architect of the San Antonio River Walk, to name a few. The National Cemetery contains the remains of more than 300 Buffalo Soldiers, African-Americans who served during the Indian Wars. San Fernando Cemetery Number Two covers 92 acres of land on San Antonio's West Side. Founded in 1921, the cemetery hosts the remains of Congressman Henry B. Gonzalez and thousands more of San Antonio's citizens. At the end of October/beginning of November, the Aztec tradition of the Day of the Dead (El Día de los Muertos), which celebrates the lives of departed loved ones, is alive and well in the Alamo City. You will find family members spiffing up the graves of their friends and relatives at this time of year and Día de los Muertos events are hosted throughout town.

East Side Cemeteries
517 Paso Hondo at South Monumental
cem.va.gov/cems/nchp/sanantonio.asp

San Fernando Cemetery Number Two
746 Castroville Rd.
satodayscatholic.org/catholic-cemeteries-of-san-antonio

Day of the Dead Celebrations

SAY Sí's Muertitos Fest
saysi.org/muertitos-fest

Esperanza Center's Día de Los Muertos Celebration
esperanzacenter.org/esperanza-projects/dia-de-los-muertos-celebration

Market Square's Día de los Muertos Celebration
marketsquaresa.com/Whats-Happening/Event-Details

La Villita's Día de los Muertos Celebration
visitsanantonio.com/event/day-of-the-dead-la-villita-activations

Hemisfair's Muertos Fest
hemisfair.org/event/dia-de-los-muertos-at-hemisfair

Day of the Dead San Antonio River Parade
dayofthedeadsa.com

19
EXPLORE YOUR HERITAGE AT THE INSTITUTE OF TEXAN CULTURES

The University of Texas at San Antonio's Institute of Texan Cultures celebrates the diverse ethnicities and settlement groups that have made Texas great: Belgian, Swiss, Filipino, Hungarian, Polish, Wendish, German, Irish, Jewish, Lebanese, Syrian, Anglo, Chinese, Dutch, English, French, Greek, Italian, Scottish, Czech, Japanese, Native American, Tejano, African-American, Danish, Norwegian, Swedish, Spanish and Mexican. Hour-long guided tours of the ITC museum are available to the public along with an archive, library and photo collection for family history research. The ITC is open Thursdays through Sundays from 10 a.m. until 4 p.m. Admission by donation.

801 E. César E. Chávez Blvd.
(210) 485-2300
texancultures.com

20

EXPERIENCE THE PASO DE LA MUERTE (DEATH PASS) AT THE CHARREADA

The San Antonio Charros (horsemen) have been on the banks of the San Antonio River near Mission San Jose since 1947. Their goal is to pass along a love for the charrería, the grandfather of rodeo. Both male and female teams compete in charreadas, which take place April through November on Sunday afternoons. Admission is $20 for adults and free for children 12 and under. Food and drink are available for purchase in the arena. During the 3-hour rodeo, you will experience the "Marcha Zacatecas," where the teams and the queen are presented to the audience and judges; the "Cala," showing the agility of the horses; the charreada, or bull and bronc riding as well as team roping; and finally, the "Paso de la Muerte" (death pass), where the charro rides his bareback horse and attempts to jump on a wild horse and tame it. Now that's something you don't see every day.

6126 Padre Drive
facebook.com/sacharros

21

LOOKING FOR LOVE? ASK
SAINT ANTHONY DE PADUA FOR HELP!

San Antonio, Texas, is named for St. Anthony of Padua. For those in the know, St. Anthony is the go-to guy for finding lost or stolen items. What you may not know is that St. Anthony is also the go-to guy for finding your true love. In Guatemala, singles flock to area churches on St. Anthony's Feast Day, June 13, to ask him for help in finding their better half. It just so happens that I was in Antigua, Guatemala, on St. Anthony's Feast Day back in 1992. The woman I was boarding with sent me to the church across the street to have a chat with St. Anthony and to place thirteen coins in his offering box. Is it a coincidence that my boyfriend showed up two weeks later with an engagement ring that sparkled with thirteen diamonds? I don't think so. Residents of and visitors to San Antonio may connect with St. Anthony right here in the Alamo City. St. Anthony de Padua Catholic Church was founded to serve the workers and neighbors of Cementville, the area surrounding the Alamo Cement Company's quarry, home of the current Alamo Quarry Market. Inside the church, which also holds a special devotion to Our Lady of Guadalupe, you'll find a relic of St. Anthony encased in a marble stand. Look below the St. Anthony statue to the left of the altar. The prayer chapel out front is the original 1927 church. Outdoor Stations of Cross by the legendary Dionisio Rodriguez, a concrete artisan, beckon visitors.

102 Lorenz Road
(210) 824-1743
stanthonydepadua.org

22
CONNECT WITH NATURE AT THE
SAN ANTONIO BOTANICAL GARDEN

The San Antonio Botanical Garden is a must-see for both visitors and natives. Even those with the blackest of thumbs will come away hopeful. The 38-acre spread will give you a taste of Japan, deserts, South Texas, the East Texas Piney Woods, and the Texas Hill Country without having to spend money on gas to get there. A new Family Adventure Garden provides 15 distinct spaces for unstructured play and exploration. The garden's Bird Watch Pavilion, given by Bill, Bob and Elizabeth Lende in honor of John C. and Sidney Helen Holmgreen, provides a quiet space to observe our feathered friends. Maybe it's because I grew up in Southeast Texas, but the East Texas Piney Woods area is my favorite spot in the garden. (The Japanese Garden runs a close second.) If you only have only a limited amount of time to explore, be sure this soothing, pine-scented area is on your agenda. Sit for a spell on the porch of the East Texas Cabin and gaze at the sunning turtles, lounging on logs in the tranquil pond. The garden is open seven days per week.

555 Funston Place
(210) 536-1400
sabot.org

23

EXPERIENCE THE MAJESTIC PEACEFULNESS OF THE BASILICA OF THE LITTLE FLOWER

San Antonio's Basilica of the National Shrine of the Little Flower is one of only 92 basilicas in the United States of America. Built during the Great Depression and named for Saint Thérèse of Lisieux, you can't miss the bright yellow spires of the Basilica from Interstate 10 when leaving or entering downtown. Located on the corner of Culebra at Zarzamora, the Roman Catholic church rises majestically above the West Side of San Antonio. Inside, visitors will feel a sense of awe and wonder. St. Thérèse believed that we should do everything in life out of our love for God and our neighbors without expecting any reward or recognition in return. "Miss no single opportunity of making some small sacrifice, here by a smiling look, there by a kindly word; always doing the smallest right and doing it all for love," she said. Daily Masses at the Basilica are at noon. Mass on Saturday is at 5:30 p.m. (Vigil). Sunday Masses are at 8 a.m. (English), 10 a.m. (Spanish), noon (English), and 5:30 p.m. (Spanish).

1715 N. Zarzamora
(210) 735-9126
littleflowerbasilica.org

24
STEP INTO HISTORY AT
THREE DOWNTOWN SITES

This is cheating, perhaps, but I'm giving you this as a three-for-one item since they are all a stone's throw from each other and can be visited in one fell swoop. (You may also want to include the Spanish Governor's Palace during this visit, so four-for-one!) The zero mile marker for the Old Spanish Trail sits on city hall's square. This movement was organized in the 1920s to promote a paved highway across the southern portion of the U.S. It's now known as Interstate 10. The other zero mile markers are in San Diego, California, and St. Augustine, Florida. Famed short story writer O. Henry—William Sydney Porter—lived in a tiny house on the corner of Dolorosa at Laredo in 1885 when he was twenty three years old. Two of his stories, "A Fog in Santone" and "The Higher Abdication," are set in the Alamo City. The Casa Navarro State Historic Site was the adobe and limestone home of José Antonio Navarro, a signer of the Declaration of Independence for Texas. Visitors will learn about the life and times of this Tejano patriot.

oldspanishtrailcentennial.com
ohenryhouse.org
visitcasanavarro.com

25

MORE THAN LIONS AND TIGERS AND BEARS AT THE SAN ANTONIO ZOO AND AQUARIUM

One of my fondest memories of the San Antonio Zoo and Aquarium is a sleepless night spent camping out with a kinkajou, a nocturnal Brazilian rainforest mammal, and my daughter's Girl Scout troop. I've always thought the San Antonio Zoo and Aquarium is one of the Alamo City's best destinations. America's oldest children's amusement park, Kiddie Park, moved to the zoo in 2019. Its original rides from 1925 were preserved to the delight of generations of park aficionados. In the zoo, the Africa Live! area is a fabulous way to "visit" the African continent to learn about its majestic animals and conservation issues. Other highlights of the 56-acre park include Kronkosky's Tiny Tot Play Spot, John and Greli Less Butterfly Rainforest, Kangaroo Crossing, Neotropica, Lory Landing, Wild Australia, the Hixon Bird House, the Friedrich Aquarium, and the Zootennial Carousel. Seven days a week, you may watch zookeepers feed condors, elephants and hippos. It will take you more than one day to see all nine thousand of the zoo's amphibians, birds, reptiles and mammals, so grab a map and and wear comfortable walking shoes.

3903 N. St. Mary's Street
(210) 734-7184
sazoo.org

26

LEARN ABOUT COWBOYS, TEXAS WILDLIFE, PREHISTORIC PEOPLE, AND DINOSAURS

A visit to the Witte Museum is a journey through Texas over millions of years and hundreds of thousands of miles. While there, you will marvel at dinosaur skeletons, witness how people lived thousands of years ago, and explore wildlife from the vast regions of Texas in the Susan Naylor Center. World-renowned traveling exhibitions are hosted in the Kathleen and Curtis Gunn Gallery and the Mays Family Center while special events and celebrations take place in the new Dawson Family Hall and the Mays Family Center. You will learn about the history and people of this region in the Robert J. and Helen C. Kleberg South Texas Heritage Center. At the H-E-B Body Adventure powered by University Health System, you will discover the importance of Health IQ, Empowerment and Wellness. Treasures of the Witte's collection, like paintings by Julian Onderdonk, Porfirio Salinas, José Arpa, Mary Bonner, and William Aiken Walker, are on display in the B. Naylor Morton Research and Collections Center. Don't miss a Gallery Theater play in the Will Smith Amphitheater or a walk around the six major gardens along the San Antonio River. The Witte Museum is where nature, science, and culture meet! Put this Smithsonian-affiliated museum on your must-do list.

3801 Broadway
(210) 357-1900
wittemuseum.org

27

EXPLORE SAN ANTONIO'S IVORY TOWERS

San Antonio is the seventh largest city in America, and it has more than a dozen institutions of higher learning that befit its size: the Alamo Colleges (Northeast Lakeview College, Northwest Vista College, Palo Alto College, San Antonio College, and St. Philip's College), Our Lady of the Lake University, Trinity University, St. Mary's University, Texas A&M University-San Antonio, University of the Incarnate Word, University of Texas at San Antonio, UT Health San Antonio, and more. Each campus has its own personality, so spend time walking around. Check out the website of each to learn about special happenings, like art gallery openings and lectures, that are open to the public.

Alamo Colleges: alamo.edu
Incarnate Word: uiw.edu
Our Lady of the Lake: ollusa.edu
St. Mary's: stmarytx.edu
Texas A&M-San Antonio: tamusa.edu
Trinity: trinity.edu
University of Texas at San Antonio: utsa.edu
UT Health San Antonio: uthscsa.edu

28
MARDI GRAS? SCHMARDI GRAS!
¡VIVA FIESTA!

Fiesta San Antonio is an eleven-day citywide party every April that offers something for everyone: parades, royalty, performing arts, commemorative medals, arts and crafts, colorful cascarones (confetti eggs), cooking competitions, raspas and more. Launched in 1891 to pay tribute to the heroes of the Alamo and the Battle of San Jacinto, Fiesta now includes more than one hundred nonprofit organizations coordinating more than one hundred unique events. More than seventy-five thousand volunteers pitch in to make Fiesta happen. The flagship Battle of Flowers Parade is second in size to the Tournament of Roses Parade. The Fiesta Flambeau Parade is the nation's largest illuminated night parade, and the Texas Cavaliers River Parade is unlike any other. Floats float. Night in Old San Antonio, Cornyation, St. Mary's Oyster Bake, the King William Fair, the Pooch Parade, and other fan favorites make Fiesta something you must experience for yourself. You'll be back for this annual extravaganza! Out-of-towners and locals reserve hotel rooms along the parade routes a year in advance.

facebook.com/FiestaSA
fiestasanantonio.org

29
TAKE A WALKING TOUR OF
SAN ANTONIO'S PUBLIC ART

San Antonio is filled with eye-catching and thought-provoking public art created by local, national, and international artists. Hundreds of pieces are scattered around town, but the most art per square foot is found in the downtown area, thanks to the City of San Antonio's Department of Arts & Culture, Centro San Antonio, San Antonio River Foundation, San Antonio River Authority, and Bexar County. The city has created art maps, listed below, to help guide you and give you details on each piece. Here are some of my downtown favorites, located between San Fernando Cathedral and the Tower of the Americas, along a 1.1-mile stretch of the River Walk:

1. St. Anthony de Padua statue outside of the Bexar County Courthouse by Louis Rodriquez, a San Antonio native who also worked on the Alamo's Cenotaph
2. "El Rio Habla" by Cecilia Alvarez Muñoz tells the San Antonio River's story while connecting San Fernando Cathedral and Main Plaza to the River Walk
3. Gargoyles on the Tower Life Building
4. "Old Mill Crossing," a 1942 WPA-era tile mural by Ethel Wilson Harris
5. "Camino de Gálvez" by T.D. Kelsey of a cowboy and longhorn steers at the Briscoe

(Take time to tour the Briscoe Western Art Museum's McNutt Sculpture Garden alongside the River Walk for free.)

6. Cross Rosita's Bridge, named for the beloved Mexican-American singer Rosita Fernández, adjacent to the Arneson River Theatre, another WPA-era project

7. "Torch of Friendship" by Mexican artist Sebastián that was given to the City of San Antonio by the Mexican government in 2002

9. Another statue of St. Anthony de Padua, this one a gift from Portugal to commemorate the 1968 World's Fair

10. "Stargazer" (Citlali) by Mexican Artist Pedro Reyes

11. "The Confluence of Civilization in the Americas" by Mexican artist Juan O'Gorman, a 110-foot by 22-foot color stone mosaic created for Hemisfair

12. "Homage to Shigaraki" by Stephen Knapp, a glass glaze ceramic mural that's the largest in the world

13. "Confluence" by local artist Ansen Seale inside the Lila Cockrell Theater

14. Glenna Goodacre's bronze statues of famous Texans, including Lyndon B. Johnson, Barbara Jordan, José Navarro and more, inside the Henry B. Gonzalez Convention Center

15. Return outside to the river level and head south up the stairs through the Lonesome Dove Grotto and waterfall before continuing on the sidewalk that runs between UNAM (Universidad Nacional Autónoma de México) and the Mexican Cultural Institute, more places to take in art

16. "Grotto de San Antonio" by local artist Cakky Brawley is just beyond UNAM after taking a left toward the Tower of the Americas. At the tower, take a left and

stroll over to the niches filled with art. Since the walking tour started with St. Anthony, it's only fitting that it ends with our patron saint and local art that celebrates our vibrant city!

getcreativesanantonio.com/Public-Art/map

30
HONOR MLK'S LEGACY

Dr. Martin Luther King Jr. surely smiles down from heaven every time he sees the crowd gathered at San Antonio's annual march in his honor. It's one of the largest in the country. Each year on his national holiday, more than 150,000 people gather to stroll a 2.75-mile route along the East Side of San Antonio. What?! Choosing to march rather than sleep in on a holiday? Yes. San Antonio celebrates its diversity. Ivy Taylor, a former mayor who was the first African-American female mayor of a major U.S. city, said: "Dr. King inspired Americans of all colors and creeds to feel that we were part of something bigger, part of an experiment in democracy and freedom that had yet to be fully realized," she said. "He challenged each of us to play a role in fulfilling the promises made by the founding fathers at the creation of the United States of America: 'We hold these truths to be self-evident, that all men are created equal.'" The march reminds each of us to support Dr. King's dream.

sanantonio.gov/mlk

31

IMMERSE YOURSELF IN MILITARY HISTORY AT
FORT SAM HOUSTON

My maternal grandfather, a physician, served at Ft. Sam Houston during World War II. Years later, my daughter, his great-granddaughter, played her only year of soccer on the fields at Ft. Sam. Talk to 10 people, and at least one is bound to have a Ft. Sam connection. In operation since 1879, Ft. Sam is a National Historic Landmark, and it is one of the Army's oldest installations with more than nine hundred buildings. Geronimo, Teddy Roosevelt, Gen. John "Black Jack" Pershing, and President Dwight D. Eisenhower are all part of its history. Ft. Sam's Museum at 2310 Stanley Road is open Tuesdays through Saturdays from 10 a.m. until 4 p.m. The Quadrangle, a visitor favorite, is full of deer, peacocks, ducks and geese that roam beneath an 1876 clock tower. The Quadrangle is open from 9 a.m. until 6 p.m., Mondays through Fridays, and from noon to 6 p.m. on the weekends. Bring a photo I.D. for entrance into Ft. Sam, and bring quarters to buy pellets to feed the birds and deers. Admission is free. Enter through the Walters Street visitor gate west of Interstate 35.

Ft. Sam Houston Visitors Center, Building 4179
(210) 221-9205
history.army.mil/museums/fieldmuseums/fshmuseum/
index.html

32

CATCH THE STARS AT THE
SCOBEE EDUCATION CENTER AT
SAN ANTONIO COLLEGE

Named for Francis Richard "Dick" Scobee, a former student of SAC who became a U.S. astronaut, the twenty-two-thousand-square-foot Scobee Education Center gives visitors a hands-on opportunity to experience space. The $12-million center includes the Scobee Planetarium and the Challenger Learning Center. The planetarium is open to the public most Friday evenings with age-specific programs for children ages 4 and above that are reasonably priced. The Challenger Learning Center offers simulated missions to the International Space Station for middle school-aged students on science- and math-related field trips. The Scobee Education Center also offers free star-gazing parties throughout the year, and it offers Friday night public showings at 6:30 p.m., 8 p.m., and 9:30 p.m. Its $25,000 telescope in the Charles E. Cheever, Jr., Star Tower will bring the stars within your reach.

1819 N. Main Avenue
(210) 486-0103
sacscobee.org

33

AMBLE AROUND EL MERCADO

El Mercado (Market Square), a downtown landmark within walking distance of the River Walk, is filled with shops, restaurants, and art galleries. Situated across from Milam Park and the Children's Hospital of San Antonio, this outdoor plaza, coined "The Heartbeat of Mexico," hosts a variety of festivals, such as Cinco de Mayo, Día de Los Muertos, and Fiesta del Mercado, throughout the year. El Mercado boasts of being the largest Mexican market in the United States. Mi Tierra Mexican Restaurant with its full bar and bakery has been in business since 1941, and it is open 24 hours a day. Don't miss their Mexican fudge. Christmas lights make every day a holiday at Mi Ti's. Add in roaming mariachis, and you've got yourself a party. La Margarita Restaurant and Oyster Bar and the Food Court eateries provide additional El Mercado options for the hungry and thirsty.

514 W. Commerce
marketsquaresa.com

34

EXPERIENCE SPANISH COLONIAL LIFE AT THE GOVERNOR'S PALACE

When a friend from Spain visited San Antonio, I made it a point to tour the Spanish Governor's Palace, a National Historic Landmark located in downtown San Antonio across the street from City Hall, with him. Spain's roots in San Antonio are deep. The palace served as the headquarters of the Presidio San Antonio de Bexar's captain and then the home of the Spanish governors. Completed in 1749, it is one of the oldest residences in Texas. Don't think Versaille, though. It's very small by today's mega mansion standards. Guests will be able to tour the captain's office and home, a living area, a children's bedroom, a dining room, a kitchen and a loft. My favorite area, however, is the back patio and courtyard. The stone walls, arched patio and lovely fountain provide a peaceful respite from downtown's hustle and bustle, but the space probably wasn't so peaceful for the criminals who were hung from the oak trees. For a country that's so new in the grand scheme of things, it's nice to have a piece of history in San Antonio that pre-dates the Declaration of Independence.

105 Plaza de Armas
(210) 224-0601
nps.gov/nr/travel/american_latino_heritage/
Spanish_Governors_Palace
spanishgovernorspalace.org

35
MARVEL IN THE ARCHITECTURE THAT IS THE TOWER LIFE BUILDING

When I moved to San Antonio in 1979, the building that made me feel like I was no longer in a small town but in a big city was the Tower Life Building. Designed by famed San Antonio architects, Ayres & Ayres, and opened in 1929, the eight-sided, thirty-story downtown building gave me a New York City vibe. It still does. Positioned along the San Antonio River, I'd often admired the building's gargoyles while walking along the River Walk, but I'd never been inside the building until I took a downtown walking tour over the holidays. The lobby sported a beautiful, tall Christmas tree, but most noteworthy was its snowflake ceiling. The Tower Life's copper roof, green with patina, gives the building its character as does its one-hundred-foot flagpole that displays the American flag. When the tower is lit up at night, it demands that you take a look. For a sublime view of the Tower Life Building, stand on the Johnson Street Footbridge atop the San Antonio River in the King William neighborhood and revel in its majesty.

310 South St. Mary's

alamocapitaladvisors.com

36
TOUR PUBLIC ART IN SAN ANTONIO'S WEST SIDE

Since 1994, San Anto Cultural Arts program has identified, trained and mobilized local artists, both young and old, to create large-scale murals that enliven and help educate the city's urban core. Docent-led or self-guided tours bring the stories, hopes and dreams of the area's residents to life. The importance of education, *familia* and Chicano/Chicana culture are on vivid display. If you don't have time to tour all fifty murals, here are five you should definitely check out:

1. Educación (1994), 2121 Guadalupe at South Chupaderas
2. 8 Stages of the Life of a Chicana (1995), 1303 Tampico at Trinity
3. Mano a Mano (1999), 1927 West Commerce at North Pinto
4. Piedad (2003), 1204 Buena Vista at Colorado
5. Líderes de la Comunidad (2006), 1204 Buena Vista at Colorado

2120 El Paso
(210) 226-7466
sananto.org/interactive-mural-map

37
EMBRACE DIVERSITY AT AN
EAST SIDE JEWEL

San Antonio has more than its fair share of performing arts spaces: the Majestic, the Empire, the Tobin Center for the Performing Arts, the Alamodome, the Frost Bank Center, Trinity University's Laurie Auditorium, the Lila Cockrell Theatre, and more. The Carver Community Cultural Center on San Antonio's East Side, however, may give you the biggest bang for your performing arts buck. Why? The Carver, which emphasizes African and African-American culture, seats six hundred. In a place this size, you are able to see the performers, the costumes, and the sets without binoculars. So, for local folks who've never been to the Carver or for out-of-town folks who are looking for something to do while you're in town, check out their annual season lineup. The Carver, a five-minute cab ride from downtown hotels, is known for bringing both national and international performers in to celebrate the diverse cultures of our world. For those who are driving themselves, parking is free!

226 N. Hackberry
(210) 207-7211
thecarver.org

38
LEARN ABOUT THE CONSEQUENCES OF DISCRIMINATION AND APATHY

Since 1975, the Jewish Federation's Community Relations Council has offered Holocaust education to students of this region. Their mission is to educate the community about the dangers of hatred, prejudice, and apathy. In 2000, the Holocaust Memorial Museum opened its doors to the general public for self-guided tours. School groups and scheduled groups of fifteen or more are given a docent-led tour and the opportunity to learn from a local Holocaust survivor. Admission is free, but donations are encouraged. Learn about the Nazi rise to power, the concentration camps, and America's soldiers who liberated the survivors. An exterior contemplative area memorializes the six million who died. My father, a World War II veteran who served in Europe, would have encouraged your attendance.

12500 NW Military Hwy.
(210) 302-6807
hmmsa.org

39
GET IN TOUCH WITH YOUR
SPIRITUAL SIDE

Although San Antonio's population is one-third Roman Catholic, the religion of the Spaniards who settled here in the early 1700s, Protestant, Jewish, Sikh, Baha'i, Buddhist, Eastern Catholic, Greek Orthodox, Hindu, Muslim, Quaker, and Unitarian congregations abound to help you develop your personal value system and explore the meaning of life.

Baha'i: facebook.com/SanAntonioBahais
Buddhist: tbcwp.org, sanantoniozen.org, and sanantonio.shambhala.org
Eastern Catholic: stgeorgesa.org
Jewish: jfsatx.org
Greek Orthodox: stsophiagoc.org
Hindu: hindutemplesatx.org
Muslim: icsaonline.org
Nondenominational: celebrationcircle.org
Protestant: churchangel.com/churches-by-state/texas/san-antonio
Quaker: sanantonioquakers.org
Roman Catholic: archsa.org/parishes
Sikh: facebook.com/SikhCenterOfSanAntonio
Unitarian: uusat.org

40

TAKE IN A PERFORMANCE OR TAKE A CLASS AT THE GUADALUPE

Founded in 1980 in the historic 1940 Teatro Guadalupe that sits deep in the heart of San Antonio's West Side, the Guadalupe Cultural Arts Center hosts a treasure trove of multidisciplinary programming and classes in six major areas: visual arts, music, literature, film, theater, and dance. I took a writing class at the Guadalupe from the then-unknown Sandra Cisneros not long after her book, "The House on Mango Street," was published. Great teacher. Great class. San Antonio CineFestival, the Tejano Conjunto Festival, the Guadalupe Dance Company, the Inter-American Book Fair and Literary Festival, Hecho a Mano Arts and Crafts Bazaar, and more bring Chicano/Chicana, Latino/Latina and Native American heritage arts and culture to life throughout the year. While you're there, don't miss La Veladora of Our Lady of Guadalupe, a 40-foot outdoor mosaic sculpture by local artist, Jesse Treviño, who also designed the mosaic mural on the Children's Hospital of San Antonio across from El Mercado and the painted mural in San Antonio's Central Library.

723 S. Brazos Street
(210) 271-3151
guadalupeculturalarts.org

41

CRUISE ALONG THE SAN ANTONIO RIVER TO SOAK UP THE CITY'S HISTORY

Venice, Italy, isn't the only city you may traverse by boat. San Antonio has its own shuttle service and tours to spirit you away. Knowledgeable drivers will give you the 411 on local points of interest. Open from 9 a.m. until 10 p.m. daily, GO RIO's narrated, 35-minute cruises cost $12 per person and travel along the horseshoe bend of the river. Their shuttle service offers a 24-hour pass for $16 at thirteen stops downtown and along the Museum Reach. All of the river barges are ADA accessible. Charters are available for groups, corporate outings, and dinners. Close to fifty restaurants provide dinner cruises that may be reserved by the seat. My absolute favorite time of year to jump on a cruise is during the holidays from the day after Thanksgiving through the first part of January. Twinkling colored lights in trees along the river create a magical fairyland that will transport you into another dimension.

(210) 227-4746
goriocruises.com
goriocruises.com/Cruises/dinner-cruise

42

PAY A VISIT TO DOWNTOWN
SAN ANTONIO'S PAINTED CHURCHES

German and Czech immigrants who arrived in Texas in the mid-1800s and early 1900s built three painted churches that make downtown extra special. Immaculate Heart of Mary, located south of Market Square, is my favorite, but they are all hard to beat. Built by Clarion Missionaries in 1912, the Byzantine and Romanesque-style Immaculate Heart of Mary is filled with lofty arches set atop sturdy pillars. The real showstopper, however, is the church's interior paint. The shade of blue on the Immaculate Heart of Mary's walls and ceiling is one of the prettiest I've ever seen. It's the same green-blue that graces Our Lady of Guadalupe's mantle (*tilma*). Besides its striking interior, the church houses the original bell that broadcasted the fall of the Alamo on March 6, 1836, from San Fernando Cathedral. IHM inherited the bell after San Fernando purchased four new bells for its towers in 1904. All three painted churches deserve a visit!

Immaculate Heart of Mary Catholic Church: 617 South Santa Rosa, ihmsatx.org

St. Joseph's Catholic Church: 623 East Commerce, stjsa.org

St. Mary's Catholic Church: 202 North St. Mary's, stmaryschurchsa.org

43

FOSTER A LIFETIME LOVE OF LEARNING AT THE DOSEUM

Since the last time I visited the San Antonio Children's Museum was in 2002 when it was located on Houston Street and my daughter was in preschool, I was intrigued by all the buzz in my bloggers group from moms with children in the zero-to-ten age range. "It's our new favorite place," said one. "We LOVE it!" said another. So, I had to go see it for myself, and I now understand all the accolades. It's awesome, and it's HUGE (65,000 square feet of indoor space and 39,000 square feet of outdoor space). Even though I am not a child, I had fun skipping up the piano-key stairs, pretending that I was a member of the stranded Robinson family in the whimsical outdoor tree house, and learning about how different lights change the colors that we see. I also enjoyed chatting with a young girl who was happily engaged in creating a spy kitty mask in the DoSeum's Art Studio. The arts, science, technology, engineering, math, and literacy are all featured in this $47-million hands-on museum.

2800 Broadway
(210) 212-4453
thedoseum.org

44
VISIT THE COUNTY SEAT OF
SAN ANTONIO DE BÉXAR

The 1896 Romanesque Revival-style Bexar (pronounced 'bear') County Courthouse sits on the edge of Main Plaza, its Texas granite and red sandstone exterior an eye-catching contrast to the limestone of nearby San Fernando Cathedral. A seven-story cupula shaped like a beehive beckons visitors to this Texas Historic Landmark that's also listed on the National Register of Historic Places. A $23-million multi-year renovation completed in 2015 has the seat of county government restored to architect James Riely Gordon's original vision, including a two-story district courtroom with coffered ceilings, gilded plaster moldings and capitals, longleaf pine floors, and fifteen decorative windows. Don't forget to look down, though, when you're in the courthouse. The Mission Tile floors are a thing of beauty. While you're there, be sure to drop by the Bexar Heritage Center, located in Suite 110, to learn more about this region's history and impact.

100 Dolorosa
(210) 335-2011
bexar.org

45

RECHARGE YOUR QÌ (LIFE FORCE)
ON THE SPIRIT REACH OF THE
SAN ANTONIO RIVER

The headwaters of the San Antonio River are located in a protected 53-acre sanctuary established by the Sisters of Charity of the Incarnate Word, who came to San Antonio in 1869 to care for victims of a massive cholera epidemic. The native people called the springs Yanaguana, a Coahuiltecan word that means Spirit Waters, and they once gushed twenty feet into the air. Located near the center of San Antonio, this sanctuary provides city-weary visitors a chance to meander along trails and connect with mighty oak trees, native plants, and wildlife that includes more than one hundred species of birds. The sanctuary also provides volunteers an opportunity to restore the ecosystem health of this sacred space. Parking is ticket-free on Fridays, Saturdays and Sundays near the University of the Incarnate Word's baseball fields. Look for the sanctuary entrance near the headwaters' toolshed.

4503 Broadway (GPS: 29.4698, -98.4708)
(210) 828-2224, ext. 280
headwaters-iw.org

46

TAKE IN SAN ANTONIO'S TRICENTENNIAL PUBLIC ART

To celebrate its founding by Spanish missionaries in 1718, San Antonio threw itself party after party throughout 2018. Fortunately, not all of the celebrations were ephemeral. Public art dedicated during the Tricentennial now permanently graces our fair city. Here are five of my favorites:

- "¡Adelante San Antonio!," a three-part mural at the San Antonio International Airport created by local artists Suzy Gonzalez and Michael Menchaca, chronicles San Antonio's 300-year history and culture.

- "Alas de México" ("Wings of Mexico") by Mexican artist Jorge Marín is a gift from the citizens of Mexico City to the citizens of San Antonio. Located near the base of Hemisfair Tower, it has quickly become one of the most Instagrammed spots in San Antonio.

- "San Antonio Street Art Initiative," located under Interstate 35 at Quincy/St. Mary's, features colorful images by 16 local artists on 20-foot tall concrete freeway columns. Perfect for photographs.

- "Tribute to Freedom" by local artist George Schroeder is the tallest metal sculpture in Texas. Located outside of Joint Base San Antonio-Lackland, the artwork pays tribute to all five branches of the U.S. Armed Forces, fitting for "Military City USA," a registered trademark of the City of San Antonio.

- "Tricentennial Clock," a kinetic sculpture by Ansen Seale, is in the 1883 Roatzch-Griesenbeck-Arciniega House in the shadow of the Alamodome. The work highlights the passage of time into the future while honoring the past.

47

ENJOY A BIRD'S-EYE HAPPY HOUR FROM THE TOWER OF THE AMERICAS

My love affair with San Antonio began in 1968 when my parents took one of my brothers and me to the World's Fair, Hemisfair, to soak up the region's confluence of civilizations and celebrate San Antonio's 250th birthday. All these years later, there's even more reason to love San Antonio. Name another place where can you enjoy a glass of wine for $6 or $5.75 for beer at the top of the city's tallest building with a breathtaking 360-degree view. I thought so. Happy Hour at the Tower of the Americas is Mondays through Fridays from 4:30 p.m. to 7 p.m. If you are headed up to the Happy Hour, make sure you get in the elevator line for the Chart House Restaurant, which also happens to be a romantic dinner destination. Another queue is for the Observation Deck. O'Neil Ford, famed local architect, designed the 750-foot tower, the tallest building in San Antonio. Ford also designed Trinity University's tower and campus. Be sure to snap a picture of yourself at "*Alas de México*" (Wings of Mexico), a Tricentennial public art piece, near the base of Hemisfair Tower.

739 E. Cesar Chavez Blvd.
(210) 223-3101
toweroftheamericas.com

48
QUENCH YOUR THIRST AT THE
LONGEST BAR IN TEXAS

When my husband and I bellied up to the one-hundred-foot wooden bar at The Esquire Tavern, the gentleman standing next to us said that he owns a T-shirt from the establishment's earlier days that reads, "I got frisked at The Esquire." Frisking no longer takes place, but it's the colorful history of this place that makes for interesting conversation. Founded in 1933 on the day that Prohibition was recalled, The Esquire has been a mainstay of downtown San Antonio's thirsty crowd for more than ninety years. The owners claim that it's the oldest bar on the San Antonio River Walk, and who can disprove them? The Esquire bills itself as a Gastro Pub that serves comfort foods. They're also a big force behind San Antonio's cocktail culture, so figure out ahead of time whether you want your apéritif shaken or stirred.

155 E. Commerce Street
(210) 222-2521
esquiretavern-sa.com

49
GET ON BOARD THE BBQ WAGON

Sliced beef brisket is one place where my family falls off the eat-no-red-meat wagon. When it comes to brisket that's been smoked to perfection and sliced into thin, toothsome strips, our willpower fades away. Sliced beef BBQ must be woven into native Texans' DNA, so we're helpless to its powerful pull. Smoked brisket should be acknowledged for the best smell the Alamo City produces. If only it could be bottled and sold! Interesting fact: We have Ashkenazi Jewish Texans to thank for bringing this delicacy to our state in the early 1900s. Simcha!

- 2M Smokehouse
  2msmokehouse.com
- Augie's Barbed Wire
  augiesbbq.com
- B&B Smokehouse
  bbsmokehouse.com
- Barbecue Station
  barbecuestation.com
- Blanco BBQ
  blancobbq.com
- Nano's BBQ
  facebook.com/
  NanosBBQ
- Reese Bros Barbecue
  reesebrosbbq.com
- Rudy's Country Store
  and Bar-B-Q
  rudysbbq.com
- The Smokehouse
  thesmokehousebbqsa.com
- Smoke Shack
  smokeshacksa.com
- South BBQ & Kitchen
  southbbqkitchen.com
- Two Bros. BBQ
  Market
  twobrosbbqmarket.com

50
LEAVE NO PALETA UNTRIED

When the temperature tops 100 degrees, load the biggest ice chest you own into your car or onto a VIA bus and head on over to "El Paraiso" Original Ice Cream and Fruit Bars, also known as *paletas*. Founded in 1984, this family-owned business was the first paleta factory in San Antonio, according to Azucena Flores, daughter of Jose and Maria Flores, the owners. Maggie and Elizabeth, daughters, and Jose Jr., a son, also work at the factory and in the shop along with various uncles and cousins. The Floreses produce more than ten thousand paletas a day. Strawberry is their number one seller, followed by lemon. Coconut and chocolate are tied for third, and vanilla/raisin comes in fourth. Other flavors include banana, mango, tamarind, pecan, pineapple, piña colada, horchata, cantaloupe, cookies and cream, watermelon, pickles, lucas (sweet and sour), cheesecake and coffee cappuccino. One paleta will set you back sixty cents. You'll have a hard time finding a sweeter deal in all of the Alamo City!

1934 Fredericksburg Road
(210) 737-8101
elparaisoicecream.com

51
BITE INTO A TO-DIE-FOR BURGER

Sometimes all you need is a mom & pop burger with a side of fries to cure what ails you!

- Biff Buzby's Burgers
  biffbuzbys.com
- Chester's Hamburgers
  chestershamburgers.
  com
- Chris Madrid's
  chrismadrids.com
- Broadway 50 50
  broadway5050.com
- Cheesy Jane's
  cheesyjanes.com
- The Cove
  thecove.us
- Diana's Burgers
  facebook.com/
  dianasburgers
- Earth Burger
  earthburger.com
- Mad Mack's Burger
  Co.
  facebook.com/
  profile.php?
  id=100063702726770
- Mark's Outing
  marksouting.com
- Mr. Juicy
  instagram.com/
  mrjuicyburger
- OrderUp
  orderup-sa.com
- Sam's Burger Joint
  samsburgerjoint.com
- TJ's Hamburgers
  facebook.com/
  profile.php?
  id=100076343738014

52

SAVOR SAN ANTONIO'S COMIDA TÍPICA: BARBACOA AND BIG RED

Barbacoa, slow-cooked beef cheeks, and Big Red, a sugary-sweet bright red soft drink, is a favorite meal here in San Antonio. Ask any native their go-to weekend food, and chances are they'll tell you barbacoa and Big Red. There's even an annual Barbacoa and Big Red Festival here in San Antonio. These 10 establishments cook their barbacoa on site. Some cook it throughout the week. Others cook it only on the weekends. Order all meat or mixed (meat with fat) with a side of tortillas and a Big Red. Give Randy Garibay's song, "Barbacoa Blues," a listen while you dig in.

Top 10 Barbacoa Establishments

- Adelita: adelitatamales.com
- Los Angeles Tortillería, Restaurant & Bakery: losangelestortilleria.com
- Del Rio: delriotortillas.com
- La Michoacana: lamichoacanameatmarket.com/en/meat-markets-in-san-antonio/
- El Milagrito Café: facebook.com/elmilagrito
- Panchito's Mexican Restaurant: panchitos.net
- Pepe's Barbacoa: facebook.com/p/Pepes-Barbacoa-100057075775241
- Rios (17 locations)/Treviño's (4 locations)
- Tellez: facebook.com/profile.php?id=100064636391672
- Tommy's: mytommys.com

53

TOAST TO YOUR GOOD HEALTH AT
SAN ANTONIO'S BEER GARDENS

You often hear both Spanish and English spoken on the streets of San Antonio. We are proud of our dual-language skills that go back for generations. If you'd been a resident of the Alamo City in the second half of the nineteenth century, you would have also heard German. From 1847 to 1861, more than seven thousand German immigrants moved to San Antonio, comprising one-third of the county's population at the time. Beethoven Männerchor, one of the oldest German singing societies in Texas, was founded in 1867. First Fridays, Gartenfest concerts, Fiesta, Oktoberfest, and all the events that draw crowds to the famous Beethoven Biergarten are what keep patrons coming back each week. It's the dedicated volunteers and members who incorporate Beethoven into their lives—to prepare the food, work the food line, and pour German beer from their taps—that make Beethoven Halle's Biergarten a place you want to hang out. Beethoven is open Tuesdays through Saturdays from 4 p.m. until midnight. San Antonio has an embarrassment of riches when it comes to sitting outside and enjoying a cold brew or two. Give these a try!

Fifteen of San Antonio's Best Watering Holes

- Alamo Beer Hall: alamobeer.com
- AquaDuck Beer Garden: theaquaduck.com
- Beethoven Biergarten: southtownbeethoven.com
- Bier Garten: biergartenriverwalk.com
- Bombay Bicycle Club: bombaybicycleclubsa.com
- Burleson Yard Beer Garden: burlesonyardbeergarden.com
- Dos Sirenos Brewing: dossirenosbrewing.com
- Elsewhere: elsewheretexas.com
- The Friendly Spot: thefriendlyspot.com
- Hops & Hounds: hopsandhoundsllc.com
- Jaime's Place: jaimesplace.pub
- Künstler Brewing: kuenstlerbrewing.com
- La Tuna: latunasa.com
- M.K. Davis: facebook.com/mkdavisrestaurant
- Tony's Siesta: facebook.com/TonysSiesta

54
GRAZE YOUR WAY ACROSS
CENTRAL MARKET

Central Market is the H-E-B grocery store chain's gift to San Antonio's citizens and visitors. Just walking into Central Market makes me happy. Buying a bar of dark chocolate with crystallized ginger makes me even happier. Taking in the abundance of fresh-cut flowers and stunning variety of fruits and vegetables practically makes me swoon. A wonderful thing about Central Market is that you can snack your way across continents for free. (I'm a Spanish cheese addict, I admit.) Everyone in your party will be sure to find something wonderful to eat and drink. Choosing will be the problem. The selection is tremendous. The store also features chef-prepared dinners for one that are packaged to go for $8 to $12. While you're in the store, pick up something to bring home that'll remind you of your fabulous trip to San Antonio: a package or two of flour tortillas, Texas BBQ sauce, or pecan-flavored coffee called "Taste of San Antonio," for example.

4821 Broadway
(210) 368-8600
centralmarket.com

55
DO THE TIME WARP AT DEWESE'S
TIP TOP CAFE

My husband and I met a friend who graduated from nearby Thomas Jefferson High School in 1960 for dinner at DeWese's Tip Top Cafe. When we got to the restaurant, Tony said, "Welcome to the time warp." In all the years he's been eating at the Tip Top, it hasn't changed. Why ruin a good thing? Winnie and Pappy DeWese started the family-owned restaurant in 1938, and their granddaughter, Linda DeWese, has carried on. It gives its loyal customers what they crave: tried-and-true comfort food. Tony ordered a chiliburger with cheese and a side of their over-the-top onion rings. My husband ordered their famous chicken fried steak, and I ordered their grilled tilapia. All the food was tasty, but the onion rings alone are worth the trip. Plus, Tip Top sells icebox pies (banana or chocolate) to top off your meal.

2814 Fredericksburg Road
(210) 732-0191
tiptopcafesa.com

56
TRAVEL INTERNATIONALLY IN SAN ANTONIO, TEXAS

You won't need a passport to enjoy international cuisine in San Antonio, Texas, which has become one of America's leading culinary capitals, being named a UNESCO Creative City of Gastronomy in 2017, one of only two in the United States. Give the food at these international establishments a taste. Bon appétit!

- Azro Authentic Afghan Cuisine (Afghanistan) azroafghancuisine.com

- Beethoven Halle and Biergarten (Germany) southtownbeethoven. com/menu

- Carmens de la Calle (Spain) carmensdelacalle.com

- Chef's Table Turkish Mediterranean Grill (Turkey) chefstableturkishgrill. com

- Chica's Bakery (Mexico) facebook.com/ profile.php? id=100041637953315

- The Cottage Irish Pub & Eatery (Ireland) thecottageirishpub.com

- Demo's Greek Food (Greece) demosgreekfood.com

- Fogo de Chão (Brazil) fogodechao.com/ location/san-antonio

- Frederick's (France) fredericksrestaurantsa. com

- La Frite Belgian Bistro (Belgium) lafritesa.com

- The Frutería (Mexico) chefjohnnyhernandez.co m/restaurants/the-fruteria

- Golden Wok (China) goldenwoksa.com

- Hot Joy (Asian fusion) hotjoysa.com

- Hung Fong Chinese Restaurant (China) hungfongsa.com

- India Oven (India) indiaovensa.com

- The Jerk Shack (Caribbean) thejerkshacksatx.com
- Jerusalem Grill (Middle East) jerusalemgrill.net
- Kobams Grill (African & Caribbean) kobams.com
- Mixtli (Mexico) restaurantmixtli.com
- Moroccan Bites Tajine (Morocco) moroccanbitestagine.com
- Nama Ramen (Japan) linktr.ee/namaramen
- Niki's Tokyo Inn (Japan) facebook.com/nikis.tokyo.inn
- Paesanos (Italy) paesanos.com
- Paloma Blanca (Mexico) palomablanca.net
- Pasha Mediterranean Grill (Mediterranean) gopasha.com
- Savoureux Patisserie/SP Café (Vietnam) facebook.com/sav.patisserie
- Schilo's Delicatessen (Germany) schilos.com
- Seoul Asian Food Market & Café (Korea) facebook.com/SAseoulasianmarket
- Simi's India Cuisine (India) facebook.com/Simis-India-Cuisine-104962319547629
- Soluna Cocina Mexicana (Mexico) solunasa.com
- Thai Dee (Thailand) thaideesa.com
- Tienda Centro America (Central America) ordertiendacentroamerica.com
- Tlahco Mexican Kitchen (Mexico) tlahcokitchen.com
- Tong's Thai (Thailand) tongsthai.com

57
TASTE THE BEST TEX-MEX CUISINE

People who've left San Antonio never fail to lament the lack of excellent Tex-Mex food in their new city. The first thing they do when they get back to San Antonio is visit their favorite restaurants. Enchiladas, carne guisada, chalupas, fajitas, refried beans, rice, nachos, flautas, salsa and chips, tacos al pastor, queso, guacamole…you can't go wrong!

- Los Barrios
  losbarriosrestaurant.com
- Blanco Café
  blancocafesa.com
- El Bucanero
  el-bucanero.com
- Casa Rio
  casa-rio.com
- Don Pedro
  donpedro.net
- La Fogata
  lafogata.com
- La Fonda on Main
  lafondaonmain.com
- Garcia's Mexican Food
  facebook.com/profile.php?id=100048655521712
- Mama Margie's
  mamamargies.com
- Nicha's Comida Mexicana
  nichas.com
- Rosario's
  rosariossa.com
- Teka Molino
  tekamolino.com

58
SIT YOURSELF DOWN AT A
TABLE WITH A VIEW

The restaurants on San Antonio's famed River Walk are plentiful. The following list was crafted for your dining pleasure. Romance is optional but encouraged.

- Ácenar
  acenar.com
- Ambler Texas
  Kitchen & Cocktails
  amblersanantonio.
  com
- Biga on the Banks
  biga.com
- Boudro's Texas Bistro
  boudros.com
- Casa Rio
  casa-rio.com
- Domingo Restaurante
  domingorestaurant.
  com
- Dorrego's
  dorregos.com
- The Fig Tree
  figtreerestaurant.com

- Little Rhein Prost
  House
  littlerheinprosthaus.
  com
- Ocho
  bunkhousehotels.com
  /hotel-havana/eat-
  drink/ocho-lounge
- Ostra
  omnihotels.com/
  hotels/san-antonio-
  mokara/dining/ostra
- Paesanos
  paesanosriverwalk.
  com
- Range
  rangesa.com
- The River's Edge
  riversedgecafesa.com
- Waxy O'Connor's
  Irish Pub
  waxyoconnors.com

59
LIVE LA VIDA LOCA(VORE)

The locavore movement—eating food that's grown within a hundred-mile radius of where it is purchased—is a national phenomenon that was dreamed up by three San Francisco-area women in 2005. Being a locavore helps reduce greenhouse gas emissions and supports local farmers. Plus, the farm-to-table food tastes great. It isn't processed, and most is organic, which means uncontaminated by pesticides. San Antonio chefs have jumped on board the locavore movement. These ten restaurants make their Mother (Earth) proud:

- Clementine
  clementine-sa.com
- Cured
  curedatpearl.com
- Hash Vegan Eatery
  hashveganeatery.com
- Landrace
  landracetx.com
- Meadow
  Neighborhood Eatery
  + Bar
  meadowsanantonio.
  com

- Pharm Table
  pharmtable.com
- The Good Kind
  eatgoodkind.com
- Southerleigh
  southerleigh.com
- Sweet Yams
  facebook.com/
  SweetYamsOrganic
- Viva Vegeria
  myvegeria.com

60
FIND FOODIE TREASURES AT PEARL

When the Culinary Institute of America opened up a branch in San Antonio at the former Pearl Brewery, a 22-acre site along the Museum Reach of the San Antonio River, the food scene in San Antonio exploded. The CIA's student-staffed restaurant, Savor, features Latin and South American food. Add Allora, Arrosta, Bakery Lorraine, Best Quality Daughter, Blue Box Bar, Boiler House, Botika, Brasserie Mon Chou Chou, Carriqui, Chilaquil, Cured, Full Goods Diner, La Gloria, High Street Wine Company, Jazz TX, Ladino, Larder, Lick Honest Ice Creams, Local Coffee, Mi Roti, Park Bar, Southerleigh, Sternewirth, Supper, and Wonderslice to Pearl's growing list of restaurants, bakeries, cafes, and bars, and choosing where to eat becomes a difficult decision. As if that weren't enough, farmers and foodies within a 150-mile radius of the Alamo City set up booths filled with vegetables, fresh eggs, cut flowers, baked goods, herbs, cheeses, bison, coffee, chocolates, gelato, lavender and more every Saturday from 9 a.m. until 1 p.m. and Sunday from 10 a.m. until 2 p.m. Rain or shine.

303 Pearl Parkway
(210) 212-7260
atpearl.com/eat

61

GRAB A SLICE (OR TWO OR THREE)

San Antonio's Italian heritage is deeper than most realize. The local Christopher Columbus Italian Society was chartered in 1890, and San Francesco di Paolo Catholic Church was built in 1927 at 205 Piazza Italia off of downtown's Martin Street. Even if you don't have an ounce of Italian blood in you, we're all Italian when it comes to pizza. Here's an alpha-ordered list of local establishments that will make your life *molto bene*!

- Barbaro
  barbarosanantonio.com

- Big Lou's Pizza
  biglouspizza-satx.com

- Braza Brava Pizza Napoletana
  brazabravapizzeria.com

- Capo's Pizzeria
  capospizzasa.com

- Deco Pizzeria
  facebook.com/p/Deco-Pizzeria-100052786192109

- Dough Pizzeria Napoletana
  doughpizzeria.com

- Florio's New York Style Pizza
  facebook.com/people/Florios-Pizza/100066698080788

- Il Forno
  ilfornosa.com

- Guillermo's
  guillermosdowntown.com

- Julian's Italian Pizzeria and Kitchen
  julianspizzeria.com

- The Last Slice
  thelastslicepizza.com

- Sorrento's Italiano Ristorante
  sorrentopizzeria.com

- Stella Public House
  stellapublichouse.com

62

SAVOR SAN ANTONIO'S SKYLINE
BEFORE ENJOYING A BIEN FRIA

The Hays Street Bridge, a Texas Civil Engineering Landmark built in 1881, spent the first part of its life spanning the Nueces River west of Uvalde before it was moved to San Antonio and erected in 1910 to provide a railroad track-free crossing from the East Side of San Antonio to downtown. The bridge, composed of two wrought iron truss spans, was closed in 1982 for safety reasons. It re-opened to pedestrian and bicycle traffic in 2010, one hundred years after it made its San Antonio debut, thanks to the Herculean efforts of the Hays Street Bridge Restoration Group. Photo opportunities abound at this East Side landmark, so bring a camera. After you're done soaking up the views of downtown San Antonio, treat yourself to a locally brewed Alamo Beer just beneath the bridge. Alamo's beer garden and beer hall are open daily to the public and offer live music and food trucks. Give "Beer, Bacon & Bingo…and Brains" (bingo and themed trivia) a try on Thursdays from 7 p.m. to 10 p.m., or "Karaoke Beneath the Stars" on Fridays from 6 p.m. to 10 p.m.

803 N. Cherry Street
facebook.com/Hays-Street-Bridge-151580447463
alamobeer.com

63
SIP A BREW OR TWO AT VFW POST 76, THE OLDEST IN TEXAS

Even though the VFW Post 76 is the oldest in Texas and was founded by veterans of the Spanish-American War, it was hidden from sight until the Museum Reach opened in 2009. The post was one of San Antonio's best-kept secrets. Not any more. Strolling along the River Walk from downtown toward the San Antonio Museum of Art or from Pearl toward downtown, natives and visitors encounter the majestic 1902 Victorian home nestled along the banks of the San Antonio River. On a Friday or a Saturday night, the festive crowd and live music will draw you in. The post's canteen is open daily. You don't have to be a veteran to enter VFW Post 76 or to purchase a brew, but you will have the opportunity to rub elbows with veterans of World War II, Korea, Vietnam, the Persian Gulf, and Afghanistan and thank them for their service.

10 Tenth Street
(210) 223-4581
vfwpost76.org

64

TREAT YOURSELF AND YOUR SWEETIE TO A ROMANTIC REPAST

San Antonio is the most romantic city in the United States of America, so it's no surprise that the Alamo City has a surfeit of seductive restaurants to help turn up the heat in both new and established relationships.

- Aldo's Ristorante Italiano
  aldossa.com

- Bar Loretta
  barloretta.com

- Battalion
  battalionsa.com

- Biga on the Banks
  biga.com

- Bliss
  foodisbliss.com

- Bohanan's
  bohanans.com

- Cappy's
  cappysrestaurant.com

- Cullum's Attaboy
  cullumsattaboy.com

- Julia's Bistro & Bar
  juliasonblanco.com

- Nonna Osteria
  nonnasa.com

- Rebelle
  rebellesa.com

- Silo
  siloelevatedcuisine.com

65

CRUISE ART GALLERIES, HISTORIC HOMES, AND GREAT EATS IN SOUTHTOWN

Southtown, the neighborhood just south of downtown, came onto my radar when the Blue Star Contemporary Art Museum got its start in a warehouse along the San Antonio River back in 1986. H-E-B relocated its corporate headquarters to the area in 1985, San Angel Folk Art Gallery came along in 1989, and then came the expansion of the King William Fair during Fiesta, revitalization of King William's historic homes, First Friday art walks, the Blue Star Brewing Company, and you get the idea. Southtown was abuzz, and it still is. It's become known as a foodie paradise.

- Blue Star Brewing Company
  bluestarbrewing.com

- The Good Kind
  eatgoodkind.com

- The Guenther House
  guentherhouse.com

- The Haven
  havensouthtown.com

- Liberty Bar
  liberty-bar.com

- Little Em's Oyster Bar
  littleemsoysterbar
  .com

- Maverick Texas Brasserie
  mavericktexas.com

- Pharm Table
  pharmtable.com

- Stella Public House
  stellapublichouse
  .com

- Tito's Mexican Restaurant
  titosrestaurant.com

- Upscale
  upscalesouthtown
  .com

66
DON'T BE LIKE PRESIDENT FORD!
REMOVE THE HUSK.

Even though I grew up in Southeast Texas where Latino anything was scarce, I was raised by parents who loved traveling to Mexico and loved Mexican food. Because of this childhood experience, I pick up a dozen tamales now and again to bring home to my own family. San Antonio, unlike my birthplace, is covered up with tamale vendors. In all the years I've lived here, I've tried quite a few. My favorite tamales, however, come from Adelita Tamales & Tortilla Factory. Four generations of the Borrego family and their employees have been making tamales, barbacoa, tortillas, chips, buñuelos, and more since 1938. For $11.25, you can get a dozen bean and jalapeño tamales to go. Pork, pork with jalapeño, or chicken tamales will run you $11.75 a dozen. Pork tamales are their best sellers. All of the ingredients they use to make their products are sourced from Texas. Every three months, 30,000 pounds of corn from LaCoste is delivered to their silo. Inside the factory, the corn is cooked in lime water before being ground by volcanic stone. Their masa is the real deal, and you can taste the difference in their tamales.

1130 Fresno
(210) 733-5352
adelitatamales.com

67
STEP BACK IN TIME AT SAN ANTONIO'S OLDEST BAR

The Menger Bar at the Menger Hotel is the oldest continuously operating saloon in San Antonio's history, according to a plaque outside its front door, which is a stone's throw from the Alamo. Opened in 1859, it was changed into an exact replica of the pub in London's House of Lords in 1887. The bar's nickname, Rough Rider Bar, is derived from the time that Theodore "Teddy" Roosevelt enlisted recruits at the bar to fight in the 1898 Spanish-American War. With a maximum occupancy of sixty-five, the bar is extremely intimate. Memorabilia from the First Texas Calvary on the Border (1916–1917) are on display along with a giant moose head and drawings of Teddy. Ask the bartender for a whiskey, and raise a glass to President Roosevelt for prioritizing and expanding America's national park system.

204 Alamo Plaza
(210) 223-4361
mengerhotel.com/san-antonio-restaurants/menger-bar

68

SIP AND SAVOR THE SETTING SUN

Dearly Beloved, Here are *cinco* (five) rooftop bars to watch the sun go down while sipping an adult beverage, visiting with old friends, making new ones, and getting through this thing called life. Afterward, let the elevator bring you down. (Bonus points if you got the Prince references.) Each location gives you a different vista of our beautiful town, so I encourage you to give all of them a whirl! Wearing purple is optional.

- 1Watson
  1watsonrooftop.com
- Fairmount Hotel
  fairmountsa.com
- The Moon's Daughters
  themoonsdaughters.com
- Paramour
  paramourbar.com
- Rosario's Southtown
  rosariossa.com

69

EXPERIENCE #PUROSANANTONIO
CUPS OF GOODNESS

Fruteria La Mission is just down the street from Mission San José, one of San Antonio's five missions, so you will have to treat yourself after exploring this stunning UNESCO World Heritage site before or after. Order a $5 cup of corn and a $5 fruit cup, and be reminded—once again—of what an awesome place San Antonio is. The corn is cut off of the cob, layered with sour cream and chili powder (sugar, salt, citric acid and red peppers) and handed to you with a plastic spoon. The fruit cup overflows with watermelon, grapes, strawberries, mango, cantaloupe, honeydew, coconut and pineapple. Is there anything more summery than fruta fresca (fresh fruit)?! Die-hard fruit cup aficionados put chili powder on their fruit, but it's your choice. Aguas frescas (fruit-flavored water), nachos, Frito pie, Hot Cheetos with cheese, snow cones, strawberries with cream, ice cream, mangonadas (mango with chili powder, salt, sugar and citrus juice), chango, ruses, picadeli and piña loco round out the Fruteria La Mission's menu. No one will go home hungry. The Fruteria has a drive-through lane, but you may also order at a walk-up window and sit in their covered shelter and watch the world pass by. This South Side standout is open every day from 9 a.m. until 7 p.m. except Tuesday. Put Fruteria La Mission on your to-do list! You won't be sorry.

553 E. White at Roosevelt
facebook.com/Fruteria-La-Mission-1525906317731754

70
CAFFEINATE YOUR WAY ACROSS
THE ALAMO CITY

For those of us who don't like talking to anyone in the morning before we've had our first cup (or two) of coffee, you won't have any trouble finding a nearby spot to savor a hand-crafted cup of joe. Over the past ten years, the coffee shop per square mile density in San Antonio has improved greatly. In fact, coffee vendors are are giving taco vendors a run for their money here in the Alamo City. Espressos, Caffé Lattes, Cappuccinos, Cortados, Flat Whites, Americanos, Caffé Mochas, and more will give you just the energy you need to check off more of the items listed in this book. But first, bask in the bean!

- The Brown Coffee Company
  browncoffeeco.com

- Coffee + Culture Bakery
  coffeeculturecompany.com

- CommonWealth Coffeehouse
  & Bakery
  commonwealthcoffeehouse.
  com

- Early Bird Coffee
  earlybirdcoffeeshopsa.com

- Estate Coffee Company
  estatecoffeecompany.com

- Extra Fine
  extrafinesa.com

- Folklores Coffee House
  facebook.com/
  folklorescoffeehouse

- Halcyon
  halcyoncoffeebar.com

- Laika Cheesecake & Espresso
  laikacheesecakes.com

- Olmos Perk
  instagram.com/
  olmosperksatx

- Panadería Jiménez
  panaderiajimenez.com

- Press Coffee
  presscoffee.com

- Revolución
  revolucionsa.com

- Tandem
  tandemsatx.net

- Theory
  theorycoffeeco.com

- What's Brewing Coffee
  Roasters
  sacoffeeroasters.com

71

CATCH A SHOW AT THE TOBIN CENTER FOR THE PERFORMING ARTS

The Tobin Center is home to five of San Antonio's performing arts groups: Ballet San Antonio, Opera San Antonio, The Children's Chorus of San Antonio, YOSA (Youth Orchestra of San Antonio), and the Classical Music Institute. With the resident arts organizations in its stable and a super-sized list of outside talent, the Tobin offers something for everyone. Located in downtown San Antonio along the Museum Reach of the River Walk, the Tobin Center was transformed from the Municipal Auditorium into its current $203-million incarnation with three separate venues: the H-E-B Performance Hall with seats for 1,738; the Carlos Alvarez Studio Theater, a smaller space with up to three hundred seats seats; and the River Walk Plaza, an outdoor amphitheater that has space for twelve hundred standing or six hundred seated along with a thirty-two-foot video wall that allows events inside to be simulcast outside. At night, the Tobin's Gehry-like metal skin, the AT&T Sky Wall, lights up the center's silhouette, giving those of us who are crazy for San Antonio's annual Christmas lights on the River Walk a year-round fix.

100 Auditorium Circle
(210) 223-8624
tobincenter.org

72
GET YOUR CUMBIA GROOVE ON WITH
BOMBASTA BARRIO BIG BAND

San Antonio has its share of first-rate live bands, but if you have to pick just one to experience before you die, you must choose Bombasta Barrio Big Band. I first heard Roberto Livar and his eight bandmates at PACfest, Palo Alto College's official Fiesta event. I was blown away by their fusion of cumbia, hip hop, funk, rock, and Latin jazz. Since then, I've seen them perform at various locations around town, including Pearl's River Walk amphitheater. They never disappoint. Follow Bombasta on Instagram or Facebook or both so you don't miss a single performance. Hearing their music will lift your soul and transform avowed non-dancers into hip-shaking hoofers. Shakira will have nothing on you.

youtu.be/9923Ei6gjAU
instagram.com/bombasta_satx
facebook.com/BombastaBandpage

73
EXPERIENCE THE MAGIC OF LIVE MUSIC

The live music scene in San Antonio is strong. In addition to being able to catch major touring acts that appear at the Tobin Center, the Frost Bank Center, the Alamodome, the Majestic, the Empire, Boeing Center at Tech Port, and the Aztec, you can also get up close and personal with top-notch musicians at smaller venues here in the Alamo City. If you had to pick just five of all of the live music venues in the region, you can't go wrong with the following:

- The Cove
  thecove.us
- Floore's Country Store
  liveatfloores.com
- Gruene Hall
  gruenehall.com
- Sam's Burger Joint
  samsburgerjoint.com
- St. Mary's Strip
  stmarysstrip.com/places/#nightlife

74
DANCE THE NIGHT AWAY

San Antonio's dance club scene is rich with possibilities: techno, house, hip hop, country, new wave, industrial, salsa, bachata, merengue, and more. The three clubs you should not miss, however, were chosen with variety in mind. The Bonham Exchange in downtown San Antonio, a stone's throw from the Alamo, is a progressive, gay-friendly establishment that opened in 1981. Its 1892 building is alone worth the price of admission. Cowboys Dancehall on the city's Northeast Side is a cavernous place that reminds visitors that everything is bigger in Texas. For those who want to get their Urban Cowboy and Cowgirl on, this is the place for you. Luna is a small, intimate venue with a Rat Pack vibe. Salsa, Soul, R&B, Latin Fusion, Rockabilly, and more round out their live music scene. The music, tasty bar snacks, and affordable house cocktails make this North Side establishment a winner.

Bonham Exchange: bonhamexchange.com
Cowboys Dancehall: cowboysdancehall.com
Luna: lunalive.com

75
ESCAPE INTO AN ALTERNATE UNIVERSE

Drama. Comedy. Musicals. Tragedy. Improvisation. The Alamo City has it all. When the lights are dimmed and the curtain goes up, local playwrights, directors, actors, and techies pour their hearts and souls into revealing life's truths to the gathered audience. Notable San Antonio theatres include AtticRep, The Classic Theatre, Harlequin Dinner Theatre, Jump-Start Performance Co., The Overtime Theater, The Magik Theatre, The Public Theater of San Antonio, and Wonder Theatre. In addition to these and more, local colleges and universities have their own theatre departments. Treat yourself to a show!

satheatre.org/onstage

76

UNLEASH YOUR RIPARIAN NATURE ALONG THE SAN ANTONIO RIVER

The Mission Reach Ecosystem Restoration and Recreation Project makes me weep tears of joy. Completed in 2013, the River Walk now extends from downtown San Antonio to just below Loop 410, an 8-mile linear park that encompasses the four Spanish colonial missions of the South Side. Walking, bicycle-riding and kayaking along these wetlands are now a reality. Springtime is phenomenal. Bluebonnets, the state flower of Texas, line the hike and bike trails. Native wildlife, such as blue-winged teals, green herons, and red-shouldered hawks, are present throughout the year, with 213 bird species now identified. Keep your eyes peeled for spiny lizards, too. This $358-million urban ecosystem restoration was definitely taxpayer money well spent. For those who'd like to roll down the reach, bicycles are available for rental at the Blue Star Arts Complex. For those who'd like to paddle, kayaks may be rented at Espada Park from Mission Kayak. Confluence Park, a three-acre park just north of where the San Antonio River and San Pedro Creek converge, provides a hands-on outdoor classroom for visitors to learn about the importance of water, conservation, environmental science, and sustainability.

sariverauthority.org/be-river-proud/parks-trails/san-antonio-river-walk-mission-reach
sariverfound.org/confluence-park

77
STRETCH YOUR LEGS ALONG THE
MUSEUM REACH OF THE RIVER WALK

When my sister, good friend and I were in France back in 1990, we shared a bottle of wine with an elderly man, a World War II veteran, whose brother lived in the United States. He became verklempt while talking to us in his broken English. "Eets just so beautiful!" he exclaimed, wiping a tear from his eye. That's exactly how I feel about the three-mile extension of the River Walk from downtown all the way to Hildebrand Avenue. The Museum Reach is another hanky-producing happy cry. Thank you, city and county leaders, for making it and the Mission Reach so! From downtown, start your stroll along the San Antonio River at the Tobin Center for the Performing Arts and head north. On the way, be sure to stop in at the San Antonio Museum of Art. Pearl, The Witte Museum, Brackenridge Park, and the San Antonio Zoo and Aquarium are also along this stretch. You may also even see Mexican free-tailed bats take flight from under the I-35 bridge at dusk, if you're in town from April through October. Is San Antonio great or what?!

sariverauthority.org/be-river-proud/parks-trails/san-antonio-river-walk-museum-reach

78

CONNECT WITH NATURE ON THE NATION'S LARGEST WILDLIFE LAND BRIDGE

The $23-million Robert L.B. Tobin Land Bridge that connects Phil Hardberger Park (West) to Phil Hardberger Park (East) is an engineering marvel. It is the largest wildlife-crossing land bridge ever constructed in the United States. The bridge–189 feet long by 150 feet wide–spans a high-traffic highway, Wurzbach Parkway, and connects the two sides of this 311-acre city park in San Antonio's densely populated North Side. Coyotes, white-tailed deer, cottontail rabbits, armadillos, raccoons, opossums, gray foxes, axis deer, and bobcats have been photographed crossing at night. Thanks to the land bridge, they no longer have to risk getting run over by a car or a truck, and neither do pedestrians! My husband and I came upon a grazing deer just off the trail while strolling to the land bridge, and we spied a bright red cardinal, who was searching for lunch. We also enjoyed viewing interesting-shaped tree trunks and felled logs on our walk, keeping an eye and ear out for the more than 150 species of birds and 145 types of insects that have been documented in the park. The half-mile walk leading to the bridge–starting from the Blanco Road (East) side–is lovely and includes an elevated walkway that climbs through the surrounding trees' canopy. The Texas live oaks and the Texas persimmon trees are alone worth the visit, but the land bridge is the irrefutable showstopper. Don't miss it! The park is open from sunrise to sunset, seven days a week.

13203 Blanco Road (East entrance)
8400 N.W. Military Hwy. (West entrance)
philhardbergerpark.org/land-bridge

79

VISIT ONE OF THE NATION'S OLDEST PARKS, SAN PEDRO SPRINGS

San Pedro Springs Park is San Antonio's oldest park and the tenth-oldest park in the nation. According to historians, Native Americans gathered at San Pedro Springs and Creek more than twelve thousand years ago, and Spaniards founded the park in 1729. In 1860, Sam Houston spoke for two hours in the park against Texas' secession from the Union. San Pedro Park housed San Antonio's first zoo in 1864. In other words, the park's history is abundant. Stunning cypress trees line an inviting pool that looks like it's spring fed, but it's not. Therefore, you won't freeze your you-know-whats off like you do at Barton Springs in Austin. The real springs are visible just north of the pool, but you're not supposed to swim in them because of the potential damage you may cause. The pool is run by the City of San Antonio, and it is open during the summer months. Admission is free, but you do have to wear proper swimming attire to get in. During the rest of the year, enjoy a picnic at one of the many tables or benches in the 46-acre park. Be sure to check out the San Pedro Branch Library, too.

1415 San Pedro Ave.
edwardsaquifer.net/spspring.html

80
SAY "SÍ!" ("YES!") TO FITNESS AT SÍCLOVÍA

Síclovía, San Antonio's spin on Bógota, Columbia's Ciclovía, started in October of 2011, making two miles of city streets car-free for folks to enjoy outdoor recreational sports and activities without having to worry about being run over. Skateboarders, walkers, runners, skaters, tricyclers, bicyclers, bubble-blowers, strollers, scooters, and dog lovers look forward to this free twice-per-year event. Síclovía's slogan "Go play in the street!" should add (and parks) in parentheses. The YMCA sets up stages along the changing routes to give attendees a taste of Zumba, kickboxing, Pilates, and more. Hula hoops may be at the ready, along with giant chess boards, bubble wands, and taekwondo presentations. Some years, you can even Zumba in front of the Alamo! Kick-start your path to fitness at this fun, family-friendly event.

ymcasatx.org/programs/community/siclovia

81

PLAY A ROUND OR TWO AT THE "WORLD'S FINEST" MINIATURE GOLF COURSE

Cool Crest Miniature Golf Course claims to be the World's Finest, and who's to argue with them? Set atop the apex of Fredericksburg Road within sight of Interstate 10, this tropical paradise has been a San Antonio recreational staple since 1929. Two 18-hole courses are challenging, yet fun. I had a pretty good run until I got to hole 13, not so lucky, and hole 14, which ran uphill. Despite these two setbacks, my overall score was decent. As the encouraging lady at the front desk said when I returned my putter, "Practice makes perfect!" Harold and Maria Metzger ran Cool Crest for almost seventy years. In 2013, the Andry family took over, and they've continued in the Metzgers' footsteps. Why mess with the world's finest?! The beautiful landscaping draws a variety of butterflies and is a welcomed antidote to screen-time overload. Recently, the Andry family added a biergarten with more than 25 types of beer and wine, pads for food trucks, and a stage for live music and dancing, perfect for kicking back and relaxing after a challenging round.

1402 Fredericksburg Road
(210) 732-0222
coolcrestgolf.com

82

COMMUNE WITH NATURE AND WORK UP A SWEAT IN SAN ANTONIO'S NATURAL AREAS

Among the 257 city parks covering more than fifteen thousand acres of land, San Antonio is fortunate to have seven natural areas or preserves and one refuge within its city limits: Crownridge Canyon, Eisenhower Park, Friedrich Wilderness Park, Government Canyon, Phil Hardberger, Medina River, Walker Ranch Historic Landmark Park, and Mitchell Lake Audubon Center. Crownridge's 207 acres, part of the Edwards Aquifer Protection initiative, offers hillside vistas and forested canyon bottoms. Friedrich, home of the endangered Golden-cheeked Warbler, offers 5.5 miles of hiking. Government Canyon, a state natural area "where the Texas Hill Country begins," is located on more than seventy-five-hundred acres of the aquifer's recharge zone and has more than forty miles of trails. The South Side's Medina River Natural Area is a 511-acre preserve along the banks of what was once the official boundary between Texas and Mexico. Phil Hardberger covers more than 300 acres on the city's North Side and features a $23-million wildlife-crossing land bridge. Be sure to visit the internationally recognized Mitchell Lake Audubon Center, a 1,200-acre wildlife refuge on the South Side that has documented more than 300 bird species. In other words, grab your walking shoes and a reusable water bottle! You have acres and acres to explore.

sanantonio.gov/ParksAndRec
fosana.org
mitchelllake.audubon.org

83

GET YOUR FILL OF BRONC RIDERS AND BARREL RACERS AT THE STOCK SHOW & RODEO

If it's February, it must be the rodeo! Trail riders from across the state make their way to this Texas-sized event, rain or shine. The San Antonio Stock Show & Rodeo is one of the country's largest with an attendance that tops a million and a half. More than six thousand volunteers make it happen. Every year since 2005, it's won the Professional Rodeo Cowboys Association's Large Rodeo of the Year Award. Over a three-week period, attendees enjoy bronc and bull riders, barrel racers, and mutton busters along with top-rate entertainment, like Willie Nelson, Reba McEntire, Keith Urban, Nelly, and Los Tigres del Norte. More than $255 million has been given to the youth of Texas via scholarships, grants, calf scrambles, and show premiums since 1984. In the livestock barns, visitors can commune with beef cattle, dairy cattle, chickens, turkeys, goats, pigs, and sheep. Visitors will also enjoy an on-site carnival, pony rides, a petting zoo, and a swine sprint. Shopping and food round out the event. If you've never had a bucking bull almost land in your lap, you haven't lived.

(210) 444-5140
sarodeo.com

84
LET YOUR SPIRIT SOAR AT
MORGAN'S WONDERLAND

Morgan's Wonderland is the world's first nonprofit theme park designed with individuals with special needs in mind. The Hartman Family created the park so that people with and without disabilities can come together to have fun and learn how to understand each other better. The $36-million outdoor park features rides, playgrounds, gardens, a catch-and-release fishing lake, a miniature train, an amphitheater, and picnic areas that are all wheelchair accessible. The 25-acre park opened in 2010, and it already has hosted more than two million guests from all fifty states as well as one hundred and twenty-one countries. Its $17-million Ultra-Accessible™ splash park, Morgan's Inspiration Island, opened in 2017. Entry into Morgan's Wonderland is a bargain, and parking is free! You may purchase your tickets online.

5223 David Edwards Drive
(210) 495-5888
morganswonderland.com

85
RUN 26.2 OR 13.1 OR 6.2 OR 3.1 MILES AT SAN ANTONIO'S ROCK 'N' ROLL MARATHON

More than thirty Rock 'n' Roll Marathons are held around the world, but San Antonio's is the only one that has the Alamo on its route. The event also features a two-day Health & Fitness Expo at the Henry B. Gonzalez Convention Center. Live bands, cheerleaders, mariachis, and an army of volunteers give the thirty thousand participants the lift they need to make it across the finish line and into the party and headliner concert at the finish. Not a runner? No problem! You can also walk. Dancing is optional.

runrocknroll.com/san-antonio

86
ENJOY ONE OF THE WORLD'S GREAT PUBLIC PLACES

Hemisfair, the site of the 1968 World's Fair, is being transformed into a world-class urban park. Yanaguana Garden, the first phase that opened in 2015, has welcomed over four million visitors. The family-focused, four-acre park features a giant sandbox, a splash pad, public art, and climbing structures that invite play. Civic Park, located on Alamo at Market, features a great lawn for picnics, concerts, and small sports games. A limestone promenade and five large water features called The Springs, where visitors can dip their toes on a hot day, provide a refreshing respite in downtown San Antonio. Hemisfair is open seven days a week from 7 a.m. until midnight.

434 South Alamo Street
hemisfair.org
facebook.com/Hemisfair

87
LEARN HOW TO WALK LIKE A PENGUIN AT SEAWORLD OF SAN ANTONIO

SeaWorld San Antonio, the largest marine life theme park in North America, gives visitors a chance to get up close and personal with sea life, including penguins in their frosty habitat. If penguins aren't your thing, dolphins, sea lions, alligators, flamingos, belugas, orcas, and more are at the ready. A variety of big-production shows and fifteen rides, including the spine-tingling Great White, Steel Eel, and Catapult Falls, will keep you hopping. If that's not enough, you may want to purchase a ticket to Aquatica, SeaWorld's water park. Restaurants and concession stands are located throughout the park, but you might want to consider packing a lunch to eat outside of the entrance. You might also consider buying an annual pass or taking the VIA bus to avoid the $32 parking fee. SeaWorld is big, so be sure to wear comfortable shoes and bring a refillable water bottle. Those who live in the sea will appreciate your rejection of single-use plastic bottles.

10500 SeaWorld Drive
(210) 523-3000
seaworld.com/san-antonio

88
HOLD ON TIGHT AT SIX FLAGS FIESTA TEXAS

Six Flags Fiesta Texas is known for its eighteen thrill rides: Batman, Boomerang, Dare Devil, Dr. Diabolical's Cliffhanger, Fireball, Goliath, Hurricane Force 5, Iron Rattler, Joker, Pandemonium, Poltergeist, Road Runner Express, Scream, Screamin' Eagle Zipline, SkyScreamer, Slingshot, Superman: Krypton Coaster and Wonder Woman. For those who are thrill-ride averse, the two-hundred-acre park also offers forty other rides, a water park that includes a Texas-shaped wave pool, live entertainment, food, and shopping. Six Flags Fiesta Texas stages various events throughout the year, including Mardi Gras, FrightFest, and Holiday in the Park. To save some money, buy your tickets and parking online. VIA's #94 Fiesta Texas Express runs from downtown and will save you $32 on single-day parking. All ages, from grandkids to grandparents, will enjoy this family-friendly park that is located in a former rock quarry.

17000 IH-10 West
sixflags.com/fiestatexas

89
GET YOUR GEEK ON AT THE
BOEING CENTER AT TECH PORT

Thanks to my godson, I know the teeny tiniest little bit about electronic sports, better known as esports (pronounced E-sports). So when I read that San Antonio was opening a Tech Port Center and Arena at Port San Antonio to be able to host esports tournaments, my antennae went up. Touring the Boeing Center at Tech Port, I learned that the campus is much more than about hosting multiplayer video game esports tournaments. It's also about providing a 3,100-seat venue for concerts and conferences, a home for the San Antonio Museum of Science and Technology (SAMSAT), and a Tech Collaboration Lab that encourages tech firms and universities to brainstorm together. The inventor of the cell phone camera, David Monroe, is the mastermind behind SAMSAT. His vision was to create a space for kids to get excited about STEM (Science, Technology, Engineering and Math) via robots, coding, 3D printing, autonomous vehicles, and more. I'm no longer a kid, but I was awed by the number of cool gadgets on display, many of them hands-on. For those of us who are technology rubes, we can still hang out with technology sophisticates at Boeing Center's Provisions Food Hall and Bar, Mondays through Fridays from 8 a.m. to 6:30 p.m. with Happy Hour from 2:30 p.m. to 6:30 p.m.

3331 General Hudnell Drive
techportsa.com
boeingcentertechport.com

90
PAINT YOUR FACE FOR COLLEGE BALL

The Valero Alamo Bowl has been providing zealous fans a college football fix since 1993. The number one team of the Pac-12 Conference goes up against the number one team of the Big 12 Conference in late December or early January at the downtown Alamodome, which seats sixty-five thousand and underwent a $60-million renovation in 2017. Over the years, UCLA kicked Kansas State; TCU beat Stanford; Oklahoma State bested Colorado; and Baylor triumphed over Washington. To take advantage of the Alamo Bowl's holiday time period, the event's organizers have prepared a Bowl Week Itinerary to maximize your stay in the Alamo City. Check out their website. Whether your team is in the game or not, a good time is guaranteed. Plus, your attendance helps support student athletes. Close to 200 students split $1.1 million in scholarships, more than any other bowl game.

100 Montana Street
(210) 226-2695
alamobowl.com

91
RESTORE YOUR HEALTH AT CAMP HOT WELLS

In 1892, an artesian well was drilled on land near Mission San José that contained 104-degree sulphur water with medicinal benefits. In its heyday, Hot Wells Hotel, a 190-room resort built adjacent to the thermal springs, hosted the likes of Charlie Chaplin, Rudolph Valentino, Sarah Bernhardt, Douglas Fairbanks Sr., Tom Mix and Will Rogers. Multiple fires and years of neglect destroyed the once grand resort until James Lifshutz, a local real estate developer, purchased the land in 1999 and deeded the majority of it to Bexar County to create a 4-acre park. The same year the park opened, 2019, Lifshutz drilled a new well on adjacent acreage, tapping into the 1,800-feet below ground thermal springs. Residents and visitors may once again "take the waters" at Hot Wells. Sit and soak your feet with fellow visitors at Camp Hot Wells while enjoying local craft beers, natural wines and snacks from their concession stand. Make reservations in advance for one of two private soaking suites. Enjoyment of a private garden along the banks of the San Antonio River is included in the price of the 1-hour rental. Group rentals for up to 10 guests are also available.

5423 Hot Wells Way
camphotwells.com

92
SEARCH FOR THE PERFECT GIFT AT
FIESTA AT NORTH STAR

When the grandmother of my childhood friend would bemoan an unsuccessful shopping trip, she'd sniff, "I didn't even open my purse." This will not be your problem at Fiesta at North Star, a store whose motto, "Where Mexico is closer than you think, and Fiesta never ends!" is an understatement. They specialize in folk art, talavera pottery, Fiesta decorations, piñatas, paper flowers, flower garland crowns, papel picado, confetti eggs, furniture, wedding decorations, Day of the Dead items, Christmas decorations, clothing, and more. "And more" does not begin to address their inventory. Fiesta at North Star is not for minimalists. Every square inch of their 40,000 square foot space is crammed with something wonderful that you will want to bring home with you or give to a friend. My maternal grandmother's maxim comes to mind: "Don't buy anything you need, darlin'. Just buy something you want." You'll find plenty you want at Fiesta at North Star, and for out-of-town guests, one-stop souvenir shopping has never been easier. While you're there, take a stroll through their Día de Los Muertos Museum to learn about this heartfelt tradition.

102 W. Rector Street
(210) 801-9900
alamofiesta.com

93
FEED YOUR CREATIVITY AT LAS COLCHAS

If you want to lower your blood pressure and recharge your creative batteries, Las Colchas is the place for you. Even if you've never handled a needle and thread in your life, you'll be welcomed and inspired by this quaint quilt shop tucked away in downtown San Antonio. It's always a joy just to walk in to see what's on display. Plus, the owners, Francine and Toni, always have coffee and treats set out for their guests. What's not to like about that?! Las Colchas has fabric to suit every taste: traditional (Civil War era), Tex-Mex (Dia de Los Muertos), modern (Kaffee Fasset), international (Japanese), and more. Plus, they have ready-made kits for those who don't have a clue how to get started. I've taken four classes at Las Colchas: crazy quilt, vintage embroidery, prayer flags, and punched embroidery. From each class, I walked away with a handmade treasure to enjoy now before passing it on to the next generation. What will you make?

110 Ogden Street
(210) 223-2405
lascolchas.com

94
CHECK OUT THE WORLD'S LARGEST COWBOY BOOTS AT NORTH STAR MALL

San Antonio, Texas, like every large city, has its share of shopping destinations, but North Star Mall is one of the city's best places to part with your hard-earned cash, and it's the only place that has a giant pair of cowboy boots set out to welcome you. North Star, which is on NW Loop 410 between the San Pedro and McCullough exits, turned 50 in 2010, and it has aged well. Anchored by Macy's, Dillard's, Saks Fifth Avenue, JCPenney and Forever 21, North Star Mall has about two hundred tenants. H&M, Abercrombie & Fitch, Coach, Michael Kors, Kate Spade, Talbots, Victoria's Secret, Express, Armani Exchange, Aéropostale, Pandora, Hollister, Guess, Pink, Bisou, Coach, Louis Vuitton, Steve Madden, Apple, and more offer something to suit every age and disposition. The distance between San Pedro and McCullough is about half a mile, so you'll log a mile if you walk from one end of the mall and back, and that doesn't include detours along the way. Happy shopping! If North Star Mall doesn't quench your shopping thirst, try the Shops at La Cantera, located off Loop 1604 near Six Flags Fiesta Texas.

7400 San Pedro Ave.
(210) 340-6627
northstarmall.com

95
STEP YOUR WAY TO GOOD HEALTH
AT PEARL

Just when you think that ten thousand steps a day is enough to help stave off diabetes and heart disease, it turns out that fifteen thousand steps is what we actually need to maintain a normal body mass index and metabolic profile. Instead of enduring a ho-hum treadmill to get in your steps, stroll down the Museum Reach of the River Walk from downtown and enjoy shopping your way across the Pearl. Adelante Boutique, Bike World, Curio at Hotel Emma, Dos Carolinas, LeeLee Apparel + Accessories, Niche Boutique, Ten Thousand Villages, The Tiny Finch, The Twig Book Shop (where you can pick up extra copies of this book!), Litmus Bespoke, Rancho Diaz, and Feliz Modern Pop will scratch every shopping itch you have.

Pearl Parkway at Broadway

atpearl.com/shop

96

UNEARTH A TREASURE OR TWO AT SAN ANTONIO'S BEST VINTAGE/THRIFT/ RESALE STORES

One of my favorite things to do when I'm traveling outside of San Antonio is to visit local vintage/thrift/resale shops. You never know what to-die-for items you're going to encounter while you're on your treasure hunt. Plus, thrift store finds make much better souvenirs than ho-hum refrigerator magnets, T-shirts and shot glasses. Two vintage Paris streetscapes that I purchased in Michigan while on a massive cross-country road trip hang on my bedroom wall. San Antonio has heaps of treasure-laden vintage, thrift, and consignment/resale stores. Let the hunt begin!

- Alamo Antique Mall
  125 Broadway St.
  facebook.com/
  alamoantiquemall

- Antiques at Broadway
  5226 Broadway St.
  facebook.com/
  antiquesatbroadwaysanantonio

- Assistance League Thrift House
  2611 West Ave.
  assistanceleague.org/san-antonio/thrift-shop

- Boysville Thrift Store
  307 W. Olmos Dr.
  boysvillethriftstore.com

- Detours and Details
  1606 Fulton Ave.
  facebook.com/
  detoursanddetails

- Green Door Thrift Shop
  1030 Nacogdoches Rd.
  slecsa.org/the-green-door

- Lasting Impressions
  606 W. Hildebrand Ave.
  instagram.com/
  lastingimpressions_sa

- Shops at Blanco Roundabout
  Blanco Road at Fulton Avenue
  instagram.com/
  thejunctionantiques
  instagram.com/
  karolinasantiques

97
BEAT SANTA TO THE PUNCH AT THE ESPERANZA PEACE MARKET

The Esperanza Peace and Justice Center's Annual Mercado de Paz is only open the two days after Thanksgiving each year. Don't miss it! You never know what or whom you're going to run across when you're at the market, and it was with great pleasure and awe that I encountered Irene Aguilar Alcántara, one of the famed Aguilar sisters, ceramic artists extraordinaire from Oaxaca, Mexico, right here in our very own San Antonio, Texas. My husband and I toured the Aguilar sisters' studios in Mexico, but there's only so much you can bring back on the plane. It was a real joy to be able to chat with Irene and buy "Frida Muerta," a piece of her folk art, for a mere $20. Not all of the artists at the Mercado de Paz are from out of town. Many home-grown artists are also present. I spied an oh-so-wonderful brightly colored crocheted toque and HAD to have it, especially when I found out that it cost only $8. As I walked through the market, several people said how much they loved my chapeau. In other words, insta-compliments. See what you'll find at the market, San Antonio's remedy for Black Friday!

922 San Pedro at Evergreen
(210) 228-0201
esperanzacenter.org

98

BROWSE 'TIL YOUR HEART'S CONTENT AT THE FLEA MART

You never know what you're going to find at a flea market, and that's half the fun. The other half is a combination of people watching, corn-on-the-cob eating, and conjunto dancing. Although San Antonio has more than a dozen flea markets in the surrounding region, I suggest you head south to the Flea Mart on the Poteet Highway, just outside of Loop 410. There you will find an enormous selection of piñatas, personalized T-shirts, quinceañera gowns, religious holy cards, Our Lady of Guadalupe key chains, and leather cowboy boots made in Guanajuato, Mexico. You may even purchase your own grave marker at the Flea Mart. Ice cold beer, raspas (snow cones), and cotton candy make strolling around this paved and covered flea market even nicer. The Flea Mart is open every Saturday and Sunday from 10 a.m. until 6 p.m. Parking costs $2, but it's free before 10 a.m. Live conjunto music starts at noon both days. The Medina River Natural Area is nearby, so make it a two-for-one!

12280 Poteet Jourdanton Freeway (Hwy. 16)
(210) 624-2666
fleamarketsanantonio.com

99

EXPLORE OTHER WORLDS, BOTH REAL AND IMAGINARY

For those of us who love to read, San Antonio is a bibliophile's dream. Fiction, non-fiction, graphic novels, used books, rare books, audiobooks, coffee table books, cookbooks...you get the idea. You'll be able to browse to your heart's delight at the following bookstores. And remember, there is no such thing as owning too many books! (And books make great gifts...HINT. HINT.)

Antiquarian Book Mart
facebook.com/pages/
Antiquarian-Book-Mart/
111194575579834

Barnes & Noble (five San Antonio locations)
stores.barnesandnoble.com

BookCellar
friendsofsapl.org/bookcellar-used-book-store.html

Cheever Books
cheeverbooks.com

Guadalupe Cultural Arts Center Latino Bookstore & Gift Shop
guadalupeculturalarts.org/guadalupe-latino-bookstore

Half Price Books (five San Antonio locations)
hpb.com

Nine Lives Books
ninelivesbooks.com

Nowhere Bookshop
nowherebookshop.com

The Twig
thetwig.com

Whole Earth Provision
wholeearthprovision.com

100
HUNT FOR GARDEN FAIRIES AT SHADES OF GREEN

One of my friends goes to Shades of Green whenever she's feeling blue. "You just can't be sad there," she said. I have to agree. Shades of Green will put anyone in a good mood. Meandering pathways, soothing fountains, cedar arbors, and blooming flowers are sure to lift your spirits. It's a gardener's dream. Even if you're not a gardener, you'll want to become one. It's that inspiring. The knowledgeable, friendly staff at Shades of Green will teach you about native plants and the benefits of organic gardening while you're there. Looking for a perfect gift for your gardening friends and family? Shades of Green will have it. Be sure to put this neighborhood nursery on your feel-good list!

334 W. Sunset Road
(210) 824-3772
shadesofgreensa.com

101

RAISE A CHEER TO TACO CABANA FOR
$2 MARGARITAS

Taco Cabana, founded by Felix Stehling in 1978 on the corner of San Pedro at Hildebrand, is a San Antonio staple. With 35 locations now scattered around San Antonio, their drive-thru windows are open from 6 a.m. until midnight. Breakfast tacos, cheese enchiladas, chalupas, nachos, flautas, Cabana bowls, and more lure in the budget-minded hungry. The absolute star of Taco Cabana, though, is their Happy Hour. Sundays through Thursdays from 4 p.m. until 7 p.m., those with a valid ID may purchase a lime or strawberry margarita for $2. You read that right. Two dollars! Domestic beers are also $2. A bean and cheese chalupa will set you back $1.89, and a bean and cheese taco is only $1.79. If you can't make it in between 4 and 7, no worries. Margaritas and domestic beers are only $3.25 the rest of the time. Treat yourself and your friends to San Antonio's most affordable Happy Hour.

tacocabana.com

INDEX